11+ COMPREHENSION: MULTIPLE CHOICE

In-Depth Guided Explanations

R. P. DAVIS

Contents

Foreword

When sitting 11+ comprehension exams at top schools (be they independent power-houses, or high-flying grammars) you will notice that, although all of their papers follow the basic formula – an extract accompanied by a set of questions – the *types* of questions they ask can vary greatly. The reason for this is simple enough: a consider-able number of these schools write their papers in-house, and that means you find quirks in some papers that you don't in others. Even papers produced by examining bodies, such as the CEM and GL papers, have their idiosyncrasies. And yet, for all these quirks, there is still a *huge* degree of overlap between these various papers, because ultimately these schools are all looking for a similar set of skills.

As a result, preparing for these exams is eminently possible. We simply need to famil-iarize ourselves with the various types of multiple-choice questions that appear (including those quirky ones!), then hone the skills required to answer them.

The intention of this guide is not simply to show you what these exams tend to look like (although, as you work through it, you will inevitably get a sense of this none-theless!). No, the intention is to go a step further, and show you how to decode the sorts of questions these 11+ comprehension papers tend to ask, and how to go about deducing the answer.

Now, before I press on, I feel it is important to make one crucial thing clear: this guide is explicitly aimed at those students looking to achieve at the very highest level. Many times in this guide I use sophisticated vocabulary and ideas. I promise you that my intention is *not* to intimidate. Rather, we must remember that these are competitive exams, and so it is imperative that we give ourselves the very best chance to succeed.

Rest assured, however, that when I use these tricky words or phrases, I explain them as I go. As a result, by the time you finish working through this guide, you should have a whole new arsenal of words and phrases to help you attack papers of any kind!

How This Book Is Set Out

As mentioned, 11+ papers are incredibly varied. However, if you spend enough time and energy looking through past papers, you start to figure out what makes them tick, and notice certain patterns that emerge time and again. This book contains eight papers that have been split into four different "styles" of questioning – two papers for each style. I have labelled the four types of papers as follows:

1. The Scattershot Paper
2. The Three-Parter Paper
3. The Poetry Paper
4. The Extended Concentration Paper

The labels I've given each style should give you some indication of what the papers entail. It may well be the case that some of the 11+ comprehension papers you end up taking fit neatly into the one of these styles. However, it is just as possible that they wind up being a blend of two (or more) styles – after all, schools often tweak the style of paper they put out year on year. At any rate, I can assert with confidence that, if you are well versed in all four styles, you will have your bases covered, and be prepared for most anything.

The questions for each paper appear twice. The first time they will appear is immediately after the extract, so that students can, if they wish, have a go at tackling the paper. They will then appear a second time, but this time accompanied by the correct answers and detailed guidance.

Each of the papers includes a "time guide" – that is, the amount of time one would expect to be given to complete the paper in an exam hall. If students wish to complete some of these papers as practice, I suspect this may prove useful.

Insofar as difficulty is concerned, the first paper in each style might be described as "difficult," and the second "devilish." Again, I feel the need to reiterate that my intention is *not* to intimidate. On the contrary, by exposing students to the reality of what is in store, I believe it ensures that, when it actually comes to entering the exam hall, you feel far more at ease.

There is no *correct* way to use this guide. Some students will feel comfortable working through it by themselves, whereas some may prefer to have a parent at hand to act as a kind of surrogate tutor. In any case, the intention of this book is to give the reader the experience of having an experienced tutor at their beck and call.

Exam Tips

Within this book, you will find a good deal of question specific advice. However, there are a number of more general tips that it is important for any 11+ candidate to keep in mind:

- When reading the extract, don't rush. Some papers even set aside 10 minutes explicitly for reading the paper, and do not allow you to look at the questions until those 10 minutes have elapsed. This does not mean that 10 minutes is always necessary – but keep in mind that every school will expect you to read the passage very carefully.
- Read the questions carefully. It sounds obvious, I know, but you wouldn't believe how many times I have seen bright students lose marks simply because they have misread the question.
- If the question is asking you the meaning of a certain word or phrase, always go back and read that word or phrase in context. Remember: not only does context impact on meaning, but it can also help you make an educated guess if you do not know the answer with certainty.
- Embrace the process of elimination. It's a great way to double-check that you have the correct answer when you feel you know it off the bat. Moreover, it's a great way of increasing your odds when you are unsure.
- Even if you have no idea what the correct answer is, never leave a question blank. A guess is better than a guaranteed lost mark.

Personal Note

When I talk about my academic career, I usually talk about my time spent at university: I studied English Literature & Language at UCL, then took a Masters at Cambridge University. However, a mere twenty years ago, I was in the same position that many of my readers find themselves in: eager to win a place at a top secondary school, and faced with a litany of exams. Of course, the exams have changed a fair bit since then; but what I'm trying to say is, not only have I been teaching 11+ students for many years, but I've also had firsthand experience of it – I know what it's like to live through!

Even though I now look back on that time through a rosy lens – I was offered places at all the top London private and grammar schools I sat for – I won't pretend as though it was not at times intimidating. However, I would observe that many parts of the 11+ English exams, and especially the comprehension papers, offer rare opportunities to engage with truly amazing works of literature. That is not to say that these exams are *fun* – my memory of them is pretty much the exact opposite – but still, it is important to at least try and embrace this side of things and enjoy the challenge.

The Scattershot Paper

I have labelled the two papers that follow 'scattershot papers', because the questions are not separated by 'type' into different sections; instead, all different kinds of questions – retrieval, inference, definitions – are thrown in together, which means candidates need to be constantly prepared to shift gears. Scattershot-style papers of this kind are what many private schools employ, but they also very closely resemble the GL and CEM papers.

You will notice that the questions in these scattershot papers each have four options (a, b, c, d) to pick from. Be aware, however, that some scattershot papers will have five options instead, which makes life that little bit harder. That said, we will be looking at questions with five options a little bit later in this guide.

Paper One: The Adventures of Huckleberry Finn
SCATTERSHOT PAPER; DIFFICULT; 40 MINUTES

*This extract is taken from a novel set in nineteenth century America. In this passage, the narrator —
Huckleberry Finn — wakes up on an island just up the river from his hometown.*

1   The sun was up so high when I waked that I judged it was after eight o'clock. I laid
there in the grass and the cool shade thinking about things, and feeling rested and
ruther comfortable and satisfied. I could see the sun out at one or two holes, but
mostly it was big trees all about, and gloomy in there amongst them. There was
5   freckled places on the ground where the light sifted down through the leaves, and the
freckled places swapped about a little, showing there was a little breeze up there. A
couple of squirrels set on a limb and jabbered at me very friendly.

I was powerful lazy and comfortable—didn't want to get up and cook breakfast.
Well, I was dozing off again when I thinks I hears a deep sound of "boom!" away up
10   the river. I rouses up, and rests on my elbow and listens; pretty soon I hears it again.
I hopped up, and went and looked out at a hole in the leaves, and I see a bunch of
smoke laying on the water a long ways up—about abreast the ferry. And there was
the ferryboat full of people floating along down. I knowed what was the matter now.
"Boom!" I see the white smoke squirt out of the ferryboat's side. You see, they was
15   firing cannon over the water, trying to make my carcass come to the top.

I was pretty hungry, but it warn't going to do for me to start a fire, because they might
see the smoke. So I set there and watched the cannon-smoke and listened to the
boom. The river was a mile wide there, and it always looks pretty on a summer

20 morning—so I was having a good enough time seeing them hunt for my remainders
if I only had a bite to eat. Well, then I happened to think how they always put quicksilver in loaves of bread and float them off, because they always go right to the
drownded carcass and stop there. So, says I, I'll keep a lookout, and if any of them's
floating around after me I'll give them a show. I changed to the Illinois edge of the
island to see what luck I could have, and I warn't disappointed. A big double loaf
25 come along, and I most got it with a long stick, but my foot slipped and she floated
out further. Of course I was where the current set in the closest to the shore—I
knowed enough for that. But by and by along comes another one, and this time I
won. I took out the plug and shook out the little dab of quicksilver, and set my teeth
in. It was "baker's bread"—what the quality eat; none of your low-down corn-pone.

30 I got a good place amongst the leaves, and set there on a log, munching the bread
and watching the ferry-boat, and very well satisfied. And then something struck me.
 I says, now I reckon the widow or the parson or somebody prayed that this bread
would find me, and here it has gone and done it. So there ain't no doubt but there is
something in that thing—that is, there's something in it when a body like the widow
35 or the parson prays, but it don't work for me, and I reckon it don't work for only just
the right kind.

I lit a pipe and had a good long smoke, and went on watching. The ferryboat was
floating with the current, and I allowed I'd have a chance to see who was aboard
when she come along, because she would come in close, where the bread did. When
40 she'd got pretty well along down towards me, I put out my pipe and went to where I
fished out the bread, and laid down behind a log on the bank in a little open place.
 Where the log forked I could peep through.

By and by she come along, and she drifted in so close that they could a run out a
plank and walked ashore. Most everybody was on the boat. Pap, and Judge
45 Thatcher, and Bessie Thatcher, and Jo Harper, and Tom Sawyer, and his old Aunt
Polly, and Sid and Mary, and plenty more. Everybody was talking about the murder,
but the captain broke in and says:

"Look sharp, now; the current sets in the closest here, and maybe he's washed ashore
and got tangled amongst the brush at the water's edge. I hope so, anyway."

50 I didn't hope so. They all crowded up and leaned over the rails, nearly in my face,
and kept still, watching with all their might. I could see them first-rate, but they
couldn't see me.

"Stand away!" and the cannon let off such a blast right before me that it made me
deef with the noise and pretty near blind with the smoke, and I judged I was gone. If
55 they'd a had some bullets in, I reckon they'd a got the corpse they was after. Well, I
see I warn't hurt, thanks to goodness. The boat floated on and went out of sight
around the shoulder of the island. I could hear the booming now and then, further

and further off, and by and by, after an hour, I didn't hear it no more. The island was three mile long. I judged they had got to the foot, and was giving it up. But they didn't
60   yet a while. They turned around the foot of the island and started up the channel on the Missouri side, under steam, and booming once in a while as they went. I crossed over to that side and watched them. When they got abreast the head of the island they quit shooting and dropped over to the Missouri shore and went home to the town.

65   I knowed I was all right now. Nobody else would come a-hunting after me. I got my traps out of the canoe and made me a nice camp in the thick woods. I made a kind of a tent out of my blankets to put my things under so the rain couldn't get at them. I catched a catfish and haggled him open with my saw, and towards sundown I started my camp fire and had supper. Then I set out a line to catch some fish for breakfast.

An extract from The Adventures of Huckleberry Finn by Mark Twain

1. Why does the narrator judge that it is after eight o'clock?

    a) The squirrels were awake and alert.
    b) The sun was too high in the sky for it to have been earlier.
    c) His sundial told him what time it was.
    d) Too much light was coming through the trees.

Answer: ___

2. How does the narrator feel when he first wakes up?

    a) Angry and irritable.
    b) Relaxed and lethargic.
    c) Abounding with energy.
    d) Exhausted and unable to get up.

Answer: ___

3. What does the word 'freckled' mean in this context?

    a) It relates to spotted animals.
    b) It relates to freckles on the narrator's face.
    c) It relates to dots of light.
    d) It relates to spotted leaves on the trees.

Answer: ____

4. What do you think the word 'jabbered' means at line 7?

a) Chattered.
b) Struck out.
c) Spat.
d) Looked.

Answer: ____

5. What causes the narrator to stop dozing?

a) The sound of a boat moving through water grabs his attention.
b) His hunger becomes too great to ignore.
c) The sound of a cannon grabs his attention.
d) The breeze causes the temperature to drop.

Answer:

6. According to the narrator, why does the ship's captain fire the cannon?

a) To get the narrator's attention.
b) To get any corpses in the water to float to the top.
c) To attack an enemy ship.
d) As part of a festival performance.

Answer: ____

7. According to the narrator, why are the loaves of bread filled with quicksilver?

a) Quicksilver causes the bread to float.
b) People believed that quicksilver would stop people from eating the bread.
c) People believed that quicksilver would stop animals from eating the bread.
d) People believed that quicksilver floated towards dead bodies.

Answer: ____

8. How does the narrator label the bread he ends up eating?

a) Baker's bread.

b) Quality bread.

c) Low-down corn-pone.

d) Quicksilver bread.

Answer: ___

9. Which is the most accurate statement regarding the narrator at the end of paragraph 3?

a) He woke up hungry and remains in a state of deep hunger.

b) He is incredibly happy that people are looking for him and hopes to be saved from the island.

c) He loathes the island but does not wish to be found.

d) He feels relaxed and easy on the island and does not wish to be found.

Answer: ___

10. Which phrase best describes the purpose of the first three paragraphs?

a) To make the proceeding paragraphs seem exciting by comparison.

b) To make the island seem like a terrible place to live.

c) To set the scene and make clear that the narrator is in hiding.

d) To make the reader strongly dislike the narrator.

Answer: ___

11. Where does the narrator sit while eating his bread?

a) On the ground.

b) Where the water meets the shore.

c) On a log.

d) In the mud.

Answer: ___

12. Which of the following words taken from the passage best communicates the narrator's pleasure as he eats and watches the boat?

a) Munching.

b) Satisfied.

c) Struck.

d) Reckon.

Answer: ____

13. What do you think the narrator means when he claims 'something struck me' at line 31.

    a) That he had been hit by an object.
    b) That a thought had suddenly occurred to him.
    c) That he had experienced a sudden pain.
    d) That a memory from his past had suddenly occurred to him.

Answer: ____

14. What do you think the narrator means when he says that praying 'don't work for only just the right kind'?

    a) Praying is always useful, no matter who you are.
    b) Praying can never yield results for anyone.
    c) Prayer only yields results for certain types of people.
    d) Only praying with the right kind of words will yield results.

Answer: ____

15. Why are the people on the boat unable to see the narrator when they pass right by him?

    a) The thickness of the smoke makes it difficult for the people on the boat to see anything.
    b) The narrator could see them through a hole in the log, yet was also hidden by this same log.
    c) The people on the boat were too high up to see the narrator.
    d) The people on the boat were too distracted by conversations they were having.

Answer: ____

16. Why do you think the narrator says he 'didn't hope so' in response to the captain's comment at lines 48 to 49?

    a) Because the narrator has lost all hope.

    b) Because the captain was saying that he hoped to find the narrator's dead body.

    c) Because the captain was saying that he hoped to capture the narrator.

    d) Because the narrator simply wanted to contradict the captain, and there was no real meaning to the narrator's words.

Answer: ___

17. Which of the following statements most accurately summarises who was on the boat?

    a) Everyone the narrator had ever met was on the boat.

    b) Exactly eight people were on the boat.

    c) Exactly nine people were on the boat.

    d) More than nine people were on the boat.

Answer: ___

18. What do you think the narrator means by the phrase: 'I judged I was gone' (line 54).

    a) He believed he was about to die.

    b) He believed he had been spotted by the people on the boat.

    c) He believed he had been rejected from society.

    d) A judge had sentenced him to death.

Answer: ___

19. Which of the following phrases is a metaphor?

    a) The cannon let off such a blast.

    b) The head of the island.

    c) The boat floated on.

    d) The island was three mile long.

Answer: ___

20. The phrase 'booming now and then' contains which literary technique?

    a) Pun.

    b) Simile.

c) Onomatopoeia.
d) Personification.

Answer: ___

21. Which phrase in the third paragraph do you think might mean 'wealthier people'?

a) Drownded carcass.
b) Big double loaf.
c) The quality.
d) Quicksilver.

Answer: ___

22. How long is the island on which the narrator is currently located?

a) Three miles.
b) Four miles.
c) The length of a plank.
d) A foot.

Answer: ___

23. Why do you think the narrator feels comfortable enough to start setting up camp?

a) Because there is no rain and no sign that there will be rain.
b) The narrator does not in fact start setting up camp at all.
c) Because the ship had returned to town and the narrator feels convinced nobody else will come looking for him.
d) Because, after eating the bread, he felt he finally had the strength to do so.

Answer: ___

24. What does the narrator use for shelter as he sets up camp?

a) The log.
b) His canoe.
c) He does not use any shelter.
d) His blankets.

Answer: ___

25. What does the narrator plan to eat for breakfast the next day?

    a) Freshly caught fish.
    b) Bread from the previous day.
    c) The remains of the catfish he ate for supper.
    d) The passage does not say.

Answer: ___

1. Why does the narrator judge that it is after eight o'clock?

 a) The squirrels were awake and alert.
 b) The sun was too high in the sky for it to have been earlier.
 c) His sundial told him what time it was.
 d) Too much light was coming through the trees.

Answer: B

There are two key methods available to us when tackling multiple choice questions: we can either work out the correct answer outright, or we can eliminate the incorrect answers. However, it's often useful to use a **blend** of these two methods. This allows us to double-check our answers when we think we've found the correct one, but also allows us to better our odds by removing incorrect answers when we are unable to figure out the correct answer straight away.

Now, this particular question largely tests our retrieval skills – that is, our ability to comb through the extract and pick out a detail. Retrieval questions are some of the most basic questions you'll find in 11+ multi-choice comprehension papers, though that doesn't mean they can't sometimes be tricky – especially when the details are hidden in big, long paragraphs!

The information we need to figure out this question, however, is not hidden. It is contained in very opening sentence: 'The sun was up so high when I waked that I judged it was after eight o'clock'. Immediately, we can see that it was the sun – and its positioning in the sky – that allowed the narrator to judge that it was after eight o'clock, which indicates that **(b)** is the correct answer.

Yet one can confirm this through the process of elimination. The sentence above tells us it was the sun (not the squirrels) that allowed Finn to judge the time, meaning we can eliminate **(a)**. There is also no mention of a sundial at any point, so **(c)** can also be eliminated. Finally, while one might assume the quantity of light would increase as the sun moves higher, this is not what allows the narrator to judge the time, thereby eliminating **(d)**.

2. How does the narrator feel when he first wakes up?

    a) **Angry and irritable.**
    b) **Relaxed and lethargic.**
    c) **Abounding with energy.**
    d) **Exhausted and unable to get up.**

Answer: B

This question tests our retrieval skills, but also our vocabulary skills. This is because the correct answer in the multiple-choice selection does not use the exact same vocabulary as the author, but instead uses *synonyms* – words that are very similar in meaning to the ones used by the author. As a result, the broader our vocabulary, the better our chances of success.

At lines 2-3, the narrator reports that he was 'feeling rested and ruther comfortable and satisfied' – this is the first piece of information we need. However, to land conclusively on an answer, we also want to take into account the extra information given at line 8: that Finn was feeling 'powerful lazy and comfortable.'

The words 'comfortable' and 'satisfied' – especially when taken together – are very close in meaning to 'relaxed.' Meanwhile, the word 'lazy' is very similar in meaning to 'lethargic'. The correct answer, therefore, is **(b).**

However, it is also possible to deduce the correct answer through the process of elimination. We can eliminate **(a)**, since there is no evidence that he is 'angry and irritable'. We know he is not 'exhausted', because this means the exact opposite of 'feeling rested', so we can eliminate **(d).**

Finally, we can eliminate (c), due to the phrase 'powerful lazy'. Here 'powerful' is being used not as an adjective – it is not saying that Finn is feeling powerful – but instead as an adverb: it is telling us the extent to which Finn is feeling lazy. The phrase, then, is similar in meaning to the phrase 'very lazy'. As a result, we know the narrator is not abounding with energy, thus eliminating (c).

3. What does the word 'freckled' mean in this context?

    a) It relates to spotted animals.
    b) It relates to freckles on the narrator's face.
    c) It relates to dots of light.
    d) It relates to spotted leaves on the trees.

Answer: C

Here we have a definition-style question. Notice that it is asking us what the word 'freckled' means 'in this context'. This is an acknowledgement that certain words have more than one meaning, and that the context can give us a clue as to which meaning the author is going with.

My advice? Although not all definition-style questions use the phrase 'in this context', I would suggest always keeping in mind how context might impact meaning.

Now, the first step is to re-read how the word is used in the extract: 'There was freckled places on the ground where the light sifted down through the leaves, and the freckled places swapped about a little'.

Reading this carefully, we can see that the 'freckled places' are areas on the 'ground' where the narrator can see 'light'. As a result, the correct answer is (c): it relates to dots of light.

Option (b) is trying to trip us up. Many students will have heard the word 'freckled' used to describe someone who has freckles on their face. However, while this is a valid definition of the word, it is *not* how the author is using it.

Option (d) is also trying to slip us up, but in a different way. The quote above describes how the 'light sifted down through the leaves' – in other words, how the sunlight made its way through gaps in the leaves to reach the ground: it has nothing to do with spotted leaves. However, some hasty students may well see the word 'leaves' near the word 'freckled' and mistakenly go with option (d).

Finally, there is no mention of animals in this sentence, so we can safely eliminate (a).

. . .

4. What do you think the word 'jabbered' means at line 7?

   a) Chattered.
   b) Struck out.
   c) Spat.
   d) Looked.

Answer: A

To my mind, 'jabbered' means to talk in a quick and incomprehensible way. However, none of the four options perfectly capture this.

I find when dealing with multiple choice questions that it sometimes helps to think of the mission not as one of finding the correct answer, but as one of finding the best answer of the choices available. Remember, while examiners may seem scary, they are human beings, and sometimes their questions are not completely and utterly perfect. (In fact – though this is very, very rare – I have even on occasion seen outright mistakes in 11+ papers!).

Let's look at the word 'jabbered' in the context Mark Twain (the extract's author!) uses it: 'A couple of squirrels set on a limb and jabbered at me very friendly.'

We know the squirrels' jabbering is described as 'very friendly'. This allows us to confidently eliminate options (**b**) and (**c**), because to strike out at someone means to hit them, which is not something associated with friendly behaviour – and the same goes for spitting at someone.

The word 'looked' *would* be able to replace the word 'jabbered' in this sentence in a way that makes sense; however, we know the word 'jabbered' means to talk in an incomprehensible way, and 'chattered' means to talk. As a result, 'chattered' is a much better option than 'looked' – ergo (**a**) is the correct answer.

(Oh, and ergo is Latin for therefore!)

5. What causes the narrator to stop dozing?

   a) The sound of a boat moving through water grabs his attention.
   b) His hunger becomes too great to ignore.
   c) The sound of a cannon grabs his attention.

d) The breeze causes the temperature to drop.

Answer: C

Again, we are back in retrieval territory: we need to comb the extract carefully for the correct information.

At lines 9-10, we are told what causes Finn to wake up from his doze: 'Well, I was dozing off again when I thinks I hears a deep sound of "boom!" away up the river.'

Immediately, this allows us to eliminate **(b)** and **(d)**, since we know it was a noise that caused the narrator to stop dozing, *not* his hunger or a change in temperature.

The word 'boom' itself is something we would associate with gunfire or cannon fire, and thus many students will likely already be able to tell that the correct answer is **(c)** as opposed to **(a)**. However, this is confirmed when, after another appearance of the word 'boom', the narrator notes that 'they was firing cannon over the water'.

6. According to the narrator, why does the ship's captain fire the cannon?

    a) To get the narrator's attention.
    b) To get any corpses in the water to float to the top.
    c) To attack an enemy ship.
    d) As part of a festival performance.

Answer: B

This is another retrieval question. The key quote is at lines 14-15: 'You see, they was firing cannon over the water, trying to make my carcass come to the top'. According to the narrator, as this quote shows, the cannon was fired to try to get any corpses in the water – namely, Finn's corpse – to rise to the top. The correct answer, then, is **(b)**.

Options **(c)** and **(d)** are easy enough to eliminate: there is no mention of either an enemy ship or a festival. While the sound of the cannon does get the narrator's attention, this is not why it was fired by the captain, and thus **(a)** can be eliminated, too.

7. According to the narrator, why are the loaves of bread filled with quicksilver?

a) Quicksilver causes the bread to float.
b) People believed that quicksilver would stop people from eating
the bread.
c) People believed that quicksilver would stop animals from eating
the bread.
d) People believed that quicksilver floated towards dead bodies.

Answer: D

Again, this is another retrieval-style question.

The key quote is at lines 20-21: '…they always put quicksilver in loaves of bread and float them off, because they always go right to the drownded carcass and stop there'. Here, the narrator tells us explicitly that quicksilver is placed in bread due to the belief that that bread will then float towards any dead body ('drowned carcass'). As a result, **(d)** is the correct answer.

We can eliminate **(b)** and **(c)** with confidence: there is no mention that quicksilver stops animals eating the bread, and the quicksilver is easily removed by Finn later in the passage, thereby failing to stop him eating the bread.

Option **(a)** is trying to trip us up, because – according to the narrator – people *do* put quicksilver in the bread to make it float, and we see the quicksilver infused bread floating in this extract. However, people do not put quicksilver in bread *just* to make it float, and thus option **(d)**, which focuses on the ultimate reason the bread is filled with quicksilver, is the best answer available to us.

8. How does the narrator label the bread he ends up eating?

a) Baker's bread
b) Quality bread
c) Low-down corn-pone
d) Quicksilver bread.

Answer: A

The key quote to decode this question is at line 29: just after Finn 'set [his] teeth' into the bread, he says: 'It was "baker's bread"—what the quality eat; none of your low-down corn-pone.' He is clearly labelling it 'baker's bread', meaning (**a**) is the correct answer.

Although Finn describes the bread he is eating as what the 'quality eat', the bread itself is not referred to as 'quality bread', meaning (**b**) is incorrect. The phrase 'low-down corn-pone' seems to be referring to low-quality bread, and Finn is telling us that this was *not* the kind of bread he was eating, so (**c**) is incorrect.

Finally, while the bread had been filled with quicksilver, Finn never labels it 'Quicksilver bread', thus (**d**) is incorrect.

9. Which is the most accurate statement regarding the narrator at the end of paragraph 3?

    a) **He woke up hungry and remains in a state of deep hunger.**
    b) **He is incredibly happy that people are looking for him and hopes to be saved from the island.**
    c) **He loathes the island but does not wish to be found.**
    d) **He feels relaxed and easy on the island and does not wish to be found.**

Answer: D

Although this is another retrieval-style question, it's somewhat more tricky, as it is not just asking us to pick out a certain detail; it is asking us to demonstrate an understanding of the content of three whole paragraphs and how things might have changed over the course of these paragraphs.

To my mind, when faced with a broad-brush retrieval question like this, the process of elimination is our best bet.

While Huckleberry Finn wakes up hungry, we can eliminate (**a**), because by the end of paragraph three he has managed to source some food – the bread – and thus he is no longer in a state of deep hunger.

Option (**b**) asserts that Finn hopes to be saved from the island. However, at the start of paragraph two, Finn refuses to start a fire 'because they [the people on the boat] might see the smoke'. From this we can infer that he does *not* in fact wish to be found, thereby eliminating (**b**).

Although option (**c**) is correct in asserting that Finn does not wish to be found, the assertion that he loathes (hates) the island does not tally with the first three paragraphs. On the contrary, he talks about 'cool shade' and feeling 'comfortable', which does not suggest he loathes the island.

Finally, we arrive at **(d)**. Again, like option **(c)**, this one correctly states that Finn does not wish to be found. Yet it also states that he feels relaxed and easy on the island, which is also correct. Option **(d)**, then, is the correct answer.

10. Which phrase best describes the purpose of the first three paragraphs?

a) **To make the proceeding paragraphs seem exciting by comparison.**
b) **To make the island seem like a terrible place to live.**
c) **To set the scene and make clear that the narrator is in hiding.**
d) **To make the reader strongly dislike the narrator.**

Answer: C

This question is quite different to what we have seen already, because it is not asking us directly about the content, but about what we believe the author's intentions to be.

Now, people will often fiercely debate an author's intentions when studying literature. As a result, having a multiple choice question on it, where we have to identify a definitive 'correct' answer, is (in my opinion) quite strange – after all, how can we say for sure what the author's intentions are? However, questions like this *do* occasionally appear in 11+ papers, and we are here to score marks, and not to debate the examiner.

This is one of those occasions, then, where it is best to think of our task as looking for the best answer of the bunch. So let's dive in.

Option **(a)** is suggesting that the first three paragraphs function to make the paragraphs that come after it seem more exciting by comparison. Do we feel that the first three paragraphs are significantly more dull than the ones that come after it – so much so that they make the paragraphs that follow seem significantly more exciting? The answer to this is subjective; but given that there is cannon fire and the appearance of a search party in the first three paragraphs, it seems unfair in my view to say it is significantly more boring. As a result, **(a)** does not seem that strong an answer.

Option **(b)** suggests that the purpose of the opening three paragraphs is to make the island seem like a terrible place to live. Now, the living circumstances described might seem terrible to some people; but since the protagonist seems to find it quite comfortable, it seems unlikely that this was the author's intention, so **(b)** is unlikely to be the correct answer.

Option **(c)** is suggesting that the purpose is to set the scene and establish that the narrator is in hiding. The first three paragraphs do indeed set the scene – namely, the island – and tell us that the narrator is in hiding. It could be debated whether this was the author's intended purpose, but **(c)** definitely seems like a very sensible answer.

Finally, we have option **(d)**, which is asserting the purpose is to make the reader strongly dislike the narrator. Some people may like the narrator on the basis of these paragraphs, and some readers may dislike him – it's a matter of opinion. However, the narrator is not doing anything that a majority of people would consider really immoral or horrible, and his voice is unlikely to make most people dislike him; so it is highly unlikely the examiner is looking for **(d)**.

Our best answer, then, is **(c)**.

11. Where does the narrator sit while eating his bread?

    a) **On the ground.**
    b) **Where the water meets the shore.**
    c) **On a log.**
    d) **In the mud.**

Answer: C

We are back in more familiar retrieval territory with this question.

At line 30, the narrator says the following: 'I got a good place amongst the leaves, and set there on a log, munching the bread'. The narrator uses a dialect from the American south, which means he uses the word 'set' instead of 'sat', which some students may find confusing. However, once we work this out, it is clear that he is sitting on the log as he eats his bread. Ergo, **(c)** is the correct answer.

12. Which of the following words taken from the passage best communicates the narrator's pleasure as he eats and watches the boat?

    a) **Munching.**
    b) **Satisfied.**

c) Struck.

d) Reckon.

Answer: B

In many respects, this is a definition question – which of these four words are the most closely aligned with the idea of pleasure? Immediately, the word 'satisfied' – option **(b)** – stands out.

To double-check, it is sensible to re-read the relevant passage, just to make sure that none of these other words are not being used in an unusual way that complicates things. However, on this occasion, this is not the case.

Some students might be tempted by option **(a)**. However, while 'munching' food is something we quite often associate with pleasure, it does not have to be pleasurable – after all, we could be munching something miserably, and thus **(a)** is a weaker answer.

13. What do you think the narrator means when he claims 'something struck me' at line 31.

    a) That he had been hit by an object.

    b) That a thought had suddenly occurred to him.

    c) That he had experienced a sudden pain.

    d) That a memory from his past had suddenly occurred to him.

Answer: B

This question is asking us to define not a solitary word, but a phrase. Crucially, it illustrates the importance of context, because people use the expression to be 'struck' by something both literally – when they have been hit physically by something – and metaphorically: when a memory or a thought has struck their mind.

Immediately after the narrator uses this phrase, we can see that the narrator is contemplating the nature of prayer. We can thus tell that he is using the phrase 'struck' metaphorically, not literally, so option **(a)** is incorrect. Moreover, it is a thought, not a memory, that has struck him, so **(d)** is incorrect, too.

We can also eliminate **(c)**, because the thought that has struck Finn does not seem to have induced any sudden pain.

Option **(b)**, then, is the correct answer.

14. What do you think the narrator means when he says that praying 'don't work for only just the right kind'?

  a) **Praying is always useful, no matter who you are.**
  b) **Praying can never yield results for anyone.**
  c) **Prayer only yields results for certain types of people.**
  d) **Only praying with the right kind of words will yield results.**

Answer: C

This is a tricky question, because the phrase it is asking us to decode is quite unusual.

Our first step is to read the phrase in context.

Here is the relevant quote: 'there's something in it when a body like the widow or the parson prays, but it don't work for me, and I reckon it don't work for only just the right kind.'

Finn is saying that when a widow or a parson (a type of religious person) prays, it works, but it does not work for him. The final phrase – the bit we are being asked about – sees him summarising his thought: he is saying that prayer only works only for a certain, 'right' kind of person. As a result, **(c)** is the correct answer.

What is particularly tricky is the use of the word 'don't' in the quote, which makes it seem as though Finn might be saying the opposite – that praying *doesn't* work for that 'right' kind of person. The way he is speaking is very similar to the confusing linguistic device known as a double-negative, and it is something you see in certain conversational types of speech.

Think of the phrase: 'That won't do you no good'. It in fact means 'that won't do you any good', even though it is technically saying the exact opposite! This illustrates yet again why it's important to look at words and phrases in context, because the context can often shed light on the overall tone. It can give an indication, for instance, whether a character is being positive or negative about something, and that in turn can then guide your answer.

. . .

15. Why are the people on the boat unable to see the narrator when they pass right by him?

   a) The thickness of the smoke makes it difficult for the people on the boat to see anything.
   b) The narrator could see them through a hole in the log, yet was also hidden by this same log.
   c) The people on the boat were too high up to see the narrator.
   d) The people on the boat were too distracted by conversations they were having.

                                                               Answer: B

───────────

At line 41, we learn that Finn positioned himself behind a log ('laid down behind a log on the bank') and that, from this vantage point, he is able to observe the boat through a gap in the log: 'Where the log forked I could peep through.'

Later, at lines 51-52, we learn that as the boat passes by, the people on it are unable to see Finn, but he can see them: 'I could see them first-rate, but they couldn't see me.'

Taken all together, it is clear that option **(b)** is the correct answer: he is concealed from view by the log, yet can see the people on the boat through a gap in it.

Although Finn does mention that there is a 'bunch of smoke', he never says that it reduces anyone's visibility, so option **(a)** is incorrect. There is also no indication that the people on the boat were too high up to see Finn, thereby eliminating **(c)**; and we are told that the people on the boat are 'watching with all their might', which eliminates the suggestion in **(d)** that these people were too distracted by conversation.

16. Why do you think the narrator says he 'didn't hope so' in response to the captain's comment at lines 48 to 49?

   a) Because the narrator has lost all hope.
   b) Because the captain was saying that he hoped to find the narrator's dead body.
   c) Because the captain was saying that he hoped to capture the narrator.
   d) Because the narrator simply wanted to contradict the captain, and there was no real meaning to the narrator's words.

Answer: B

Let's take a look at the captain's comment (at lines 48-49) to which the narrator is replying: '…maybe he's washed ashore and got tangled amongst the brush at the water's edge. I hope so, anyway'.

The captain is, in effect, saying that he hopes that the narrator, Huckleberry Finn, has washed ashore; and, given that the captain is leading a search party that has already shown that it is trying to locate a corpse, and the fact that someone still alive would likely struggle loose of the 'brush' at the water's edge, we can infer that this is so they can track down Finn's dead body. As a result, option (**b**) is the correct answer: Finn is humorously hoping that they do not find him dead and tangled among the brush!

Option (**c**) is trying to catch out those who do not realise that the captain appears to be on the hunt for Finn's dead boy. Options (**a**) and (**d**), on the other hand, are trying to catch out those who do not take the time to re-read the captain's comments!

17. Which of the following statements most accurately summarises who was on the boat?

    a) Everyone the narrator had ever met was on the boat.
    b) Exactly eight people were on the boat.
    c) Exactly nine people were on the boat.
    d) More than nine people were on the boat.

Answer: D

This question – a retrieval-skills exercise – requires an attention to detail.

At lines 44-46, we have the following information: 'Pap, and Judge Thatcher, and Bessie Thatcher, and Jo Harper, and Tom Sawyer, and his old Aunt Polly, and Sid and Mary, and plenty more'.

This list amounts to eight people, and the captain makes nine. However, since the narrator tells us there are 'plenty more', we know that there are in fact more than nine people on the boat. As a result, (**d**) is the correct answer.

. . .

18. What do you think the narrator means by the phrase: 'I judged I was gone' (line 54).

    a) He believed he was about to die.
    b) He believed he had been spotted by the people on the boat.
    c) He believed he had been rejected from society.
    d) A judge had sentenced him to death.

Answer: A

This line comes directly after the cannon is fired again and momentarily renders Finn deaf and blind. Given the context of a weapon firing, and the fact that 'gone' is a colloquialism for having passed away, we can infer that **(a)** is the correct answer.

A colloquialism, by the way, is an informal or conversational kind of word or phrase.

19. Which of the following phrases is a metaphor?

    a) The cannon let off such a blast.
    b) The head of the island.
    c) The boat floated on.
    d) The island was three mile long.

Answer: B

A metaphor is a linguistic device in which one thing is implicitly compared or likened to another thing. A similar technical term is a simile, which is when one thing is explicitly compared to another using the word 'like' or 'as'.

Let's briefly look at the difference between the two.

If I were to say: 'The pain felt like fire coursing through my body', this would be a simile, because I am using the word 'like' to compare my pain to fire.

However, if I were instead to say: 'The pain was a fire coursing through my body', this would be a metaphor. I'm still likening my pain to fire, but this time I'm not using the word 'like' and 'as' to make that comparison explicit.

Technically speaking, a simile is a type of metaphor; but for the sake of 11+ exams, it's best to think of them as two separate entities.

Now, the correct answer to the question above is **(b)**. This is because the island does not literally have a head. Instead, the narrator is implicitly likening the top of the island to a head.

Quite simply, there are no other implicit comparisons in any of the three other options, so they cannot be metaphors. The island, for instance, is not being likened to 'three miles' in option **(d)**; it is quite literally three miles long. As a result, we can also eliminate all the other options.

20. The phrase 'booming now and then' contains which literary technique?

    a) **Pun.**
    b) **Simile.**
    c) **Onomatopoeia.**
    d) **Personification.**

Answer: C

Onomatopoeia is when you have a word that audibly sounds like the thing it is describing. The word 'sizzle', for instance, sounds similar to when something sizzles. The word 'crash' sounds like the phenomenon of objects colliding.

Boom is another example of onomatopoeia. As such, **(c)** is the correct option.

We have just discussed similes in the previous question; so the fact that there is no comparison using the word 'like' or 'as' here means it cannot be a simile, and thus **(b)** is incorrect.

A pun is a type of play on words. To illustrate, there is an old joke that goes as follows:

> *'Excuse me sir, are you a piece of string?'*

> *'No, I'm a frayed knot.'*

The phrase 'frayed knot' sounds almost indistinguishable to the expression 'afraid not' – a common phrase people say after the word 'no'. This is an example, then, of a pun.

There is no such joke in the question above; as a result, **(a)** is incorrect.

Finally, we have the word personification. This is when human attributes are given to non-human or even inanimate things. If I were to say: 'the ship was sneezing out cannon balls', this would be personification: sneezing is something humans do, yet I'm assigning the ability to a ship. However, since there is no such technique in the question above, we know **(d)** is also incorrect.

21. Which phrase in the third paragraph do you think might mean 'wealthier people'?

>   a) **drownded carcass**
>   b) **big double loaf**
>   c) **the quality**
>   d) **quicksilver**

Answer: C

The trick here is to look at each of these expressions in their contexts.

That said, some are fairly clearly incorrect. A 'drowned carcass', for example, is referring to a dead body, and is plainly incorrect. 'Quicksilver' is a type of metal and is, again, incorrect. We can therefore eliminate **(a)** and **(d)**.

The phrase 'big double loaf' could conceivably be used metaphorically to refer to wealthy people – in a similar way that the expression 'fat cat' does. However, if we look at the phrase in context, we can see that Huckleberry Finn is referring to a literal loaf of bread, so **(b)** is off the table.

In fact, we are told the bread Finn is eating is 'what the quality eat'. It is plain that he is talking about a group of people who would be likely to eat this kind of bread; moreover, 'quality' is also a word associated with wealth. As a result, even though the process of elimination has already led us to **(c)**, it is also makes perfect sense that **(c)** is the correct answer.

22. How long is the island on which the narrator is currently located?

>   a) **Three miles.**
>   b) **Four miles.**
>   c) **The length of a plank.**

d) A foot.

Answer: A

This is a pure retrieval-style question.

At lines 58-59, Finn tells us that 'The island was three mile long'. Accordingly, **(a)** is the correct answer.

23. Why do you think the narrator feels comfortable enough to start setting up camp?

    a) Because there is no rain and no sign that there will be rain.
    b) The narrator does not in fact start setting up camp at all.
    c) Because the ship had returned to town and the narrator feels convinced nobody else will come looking for him.
    d) Because, after eating the bread, he felt he finally had the strength to do so.

Answer: C

This question requires some light inference to glean the correct answer.

At the end of the penultimate (second to last) paragraph, Finn observes that the ship that was searching for him 'quit shooting and dropped over to the Missouri shore and went home to the town'.

Immediately after this, Finn says that he 'was all right now', that 'Nobody else would come a-hunting after' him, then launches into setting up camp. Although the causation is not made explicit, it is made fairly clear that he feels comfortable doing so because the search party has departed and because he feels certain nobody else is coming for him.

Option **(c)**, then, is the correct answer.

24. What does the narrator use for shelter as he sets up camp?

    a) The log.

b) His canoe.
c) He does not use any shelter.
d) His blankets.

Answer: D

This is a more straightforward retrieval question.

At lines 66-67, the narrator makes clear that he uses blankets to create a shelter: 'I made a kind of a tent out of my blankets to put my things under so the rain couldn't get at them'. Accordingly, **(d)** is the correct answer.

25. What does the narrator plan to eat for breakfast the next day?

a) Freshly caught fish.
b) Bread from the previous day.
c) The remains of the catfish he ate for supper.
d) The passage does not say.

Answer: A

In the very final sentence of the extract, Finn tells us that he puts out a fishing line, so he can catch a fresh fish to eat at breakfast the next day: 'Then I set out a line to catch some fish for breakfast'. In consequence, option **(a)** is the correct answer.

In this extract – set in a fictional version of 1950s America – Ed Loyce heads to his TV store in town after running some chores at home.

1 Ed Loyce washed up, tossed on his hat and coat, got his car out and headed across town toward his TV sales store. He was tired. His back and shoulders ached from digging dirt out of the basement and wheeling it into the back yard. But for a forty-year-old man he had done okay. Janet could get a new vase with the money he had

5 saved; and he liked the idea of repairing the foundations himself!

It was getting dark. The setting sun cast long rays over the scurrying commuters, tired and grim-faced, women loaded down with bundles and packages, students swarming home from the university, mixing with clerks and businessmen and drab secretaries. He stopped his Packard for a red light and then started it up again. The store had

10 been open without him; he'd arrive just in time to spell the help for dinner, go over the records of the day, maybe even close a couple of sales himself. He drove slowly past the small square of green in the center of the street, the town park. There were no parking places in front of LOYCE TV SALES AND SERVICE. He cursed under his breath and swung the car in a U-turn. Again he passed the little square of green

15 with its lonely drinking fountain and bench and single lamppost.

From the lamppost something was hanging. A shapeless dark bundle, swinging a little with the wind. Like a dummy of some sort. Loyce rolled down his window and peered out. What the hell was it? A display of some kind? Sometimes the Chamber of Commerce put up displays in the square.

20 Again he made a U-turn and brought his car around. He passed the park and concentrated on the dark bundle. It wasn't a dummy. And if it was a display it was a strange kind. The hackles on his neck rose and he swallowed uneasily. Sweat slid out on his face and hands.

It was a body. A human body.

— — —

25 "Look at it!" Loyce snapped. "Come on out here!"

Don Fergusson came slowly out of the store, buttoning his pin-stripe coat with dignity. "This is a big deal, Ed. I can't just leave the guy standing there."

"See it?" Ed pointed into the gathering gloom. The lamppost jutted up against the sky—the post and the bundle swinging from it. "There it is. How the hell long has it
30 been there?" His voice rose excitedly. "What's wrong with everybody? They just walk on past!"

Don Fergusson lit a cigarette slowly. "Take it easy, old man. There must be a good reason, or it wouldn't be there."

"A reason! What kind of a reason?"

35 Fergusson shrugged. "Like the time the Traffic Safety Council put that wrecked Buick there. Some sort of civic thing. How would I know?"

Jack Potter from the shoe shop joined them. "What's up, boys?"

"There's a body hanging from the lamppost," Loyce said. "I'm going to call the cops."

"They must know about it," Potter said. "Or otherwise it wouldn't be there."

40 "I got to get back in." Fergusson headed back into the store. "Business before pleasure."

Loyce began to get hysterical. "You see it? You see it hanging there? A man's body! A dead man!"

"Sure, Ed. I saw it this afternoon when I went out for coffee."

45 "You mean it's been there all afternoon?"

"Sure. What's the matter?" Potter glanced at his watch. "Have to run. See you later, Ed."

Potter hurried off, joining the flow of people moving along the sidewalk. Men and women, passing by the park. A few glanced up curiously at the dark bundle—and
50   then went on. Nobody stopped. Nobody paid any attention.

"I'm going nuts," Loyce whispered. He made his way to the curb and crossed out into traffic, among the cars. Horns honked angrily at him. He gained the curb and stepped up onto the little square of green.

The man had been middle-aged. His clothing was ripped and torn, a gray suit,
55   splashed and caked with dried mud. A stranger. Loyce had never seen him before. Not a local man. His face was partly turned, away, and in the evening wind he spun a little, turning gently, silently. His skin was gouged and cut. Red gashes, deep scratches of congealed blood. A pair of steel-rimmed glasses hung from one ear, dangling foolishly. His eyes bulged. His mouth was open, tongue thick and ugly blue.

60   "For Heaven's sake," Loyce muttered, sickened. He pushed down his nausea and made his way back to the sidewalk. He was shaking all over, with revulsion—and fear.

Why? Who was the man? Why was he hanging there? What did it mean?

And—why didn't anybody notice?

He bumped into a small man hurrying along the sidewalk. "Watch it!" the man
65   grated, "Oh, it's you, Ed."

Ed nodded dazedly. "Hello, Jenkins."

"What's the matter?" The stationery clerk caught Ed's arm. "You look sick."

"The body. There in the park."

"Sure, Ed." Jenkins led him into the alcove of LOYCE TV SALES AND SERVICE.
70   "Take it easy."

Margaret Henderson from the jewelry store joined them. "Something wrong?"

"Ed's not feeling well."

Loyce yanked himself free. "How can you stand here? Don't you see it? For God's sake—"

75   "What's he talking about?" Margaret asked nervously.

"The body!" Ed shouted. "The body hanging there!"

More people collected. "Is he sick? It's Ed Loyce. You okay, Ed?"

"The body!" Loyce screamed, struggling to get past them. Hands caught at him. He tore loose. "Let me go! The police! Get the police!"

80   "Ed—"

"Better get a doctor!"

"He must be sick."

"Or drunk."

Loyce fought his way through the people. He stumbled and half fell. Through a blur
85 he saw rows of faces, curious, concerned, anxious. Men and women halting to see
what the disturbance was. He fought past them toward his store. He could see
Fergusson inside talking to a man, showing him an Emerson TV set. Pete Foley in the
back at the service counter, setting up a new Philco. Loyce shouted at them frantically.
His voice was lost in the roar of traffic and the murmur around him.

90 "Do something!" he screamed. "Don't stand there! Do something! Something's
wrong! Something's happened! Things are going on!"

The crowd melted respectfully for the two heavy-set cops moving efficiently toward
Loyce.

An extract from Philip K Dick's 'The Hanging Stranger'

---

1. Why does Ed Loyce feel tired as he heads across town?

a) He is forty-years-old and is feeling old.
b) He has been repairing the foundations of the house.
c) He has been washing up.
d) He has been working at his TV store all day.

Answer: ___

2. How does Janet want to spend the money Ed Loyce has saved?

a) On repairing the house's foundations.
b) On purchasing a new vase.
c) On purchasing a new TV.
d) On purchasing a new car.

Answer: ___

3. What time of day is it at the start of this extract?

a) Dawn.

b) Midday.
c) Midnight.
d) Late afternoon.

Answer: ___

4. Why do you think the author describes the commuting students as 'swarming'?

a) Because they are moving in a way reminiscent of insects.
b) Because it is a hot day and they are all very warm.
c) Because the students are like parasites and sucking life out of the town.
d) Because the students specialise in studying insects.

Answer: ___

5. What do you think the word drab means at line 8?

a) Business-like.
b) Discontent and unhappy.
c) Dreary in appearance
d) Angry in appearance.

Answer: ___

6. Why has Loyce driven back into town at the start of this extract?

a) He wants to investigate what is happening in the town square.
b) He wants to organise dinner for his employees.
c) He wants to check in with his shop and try and make some sales.
d) He wanted to spend some time watching the commuters.

Answer: ___

7. How does Loyce feel when he discovers there are no parking spaces outside of his shop?

a) He is happy, because he thinks it means his shop is busy.
b) He has no strong feelings.
c) He feels irritated at the fact he will need to park elsewhere.
d) He feels regretful that he stopped for so long at the traffic light.

Answer: ____

8. Which of the following most accurately describes the town park?

  a) It contains a water fountain and a lamppost, but no bench.
  b) It contains a lamppost, a fountain, a bench and a dummy.
  c) It contains just a bench and a water fountain.
  d) It contains a lamppost, a fountain and a bench.

Answer: ____

9. Which phrase best describes the purpose of the first four paragraphs?

  a) To make Ed Loyce's life seem boring.
  b) To make the reader feel sorry for the man on the lamppost.
  c) To make the proceeding paragraphs seem easy to understand by comparison.
  d) To set the scene and introduce the presence of something unnerving to Ed Loyce.

Answer: ____

10. Which is the most accurate statement regarding Ed Loyce at the end of paragraph four?

  a) He feels indifferent about what he has seen in the town park.
  b) He feels guilty that he has not been at his shop all day, and eager to tell his staff about his day.
  c) He feels disturbed and confused by the presence in the park.
  d) He feels responsible for the dead body and feels scared of being caught.

Answer: ____

11. What do you understand by the phrase 'gathering gloom'?

  a) Pitch darkness.
  b) Increasing darkness.
  c) Increasing mood of anxiety.
  d) Decreasing darkness.

Answer: ____

12. Re-read line 30. What do you think the word 'excitedly' means in this context?

    a) Enthusiastically.
    b) Electrically.
    c) Loudly.
    d) Agitatedly.

Answer: ___

13. What do you think Fergusson means by 'some sort of civic thing' at line 36?

    a) Something educational organised by the government.
    b) Something that only members of the civil service would understand.
    c) Something that is very civilised.
    d) Something that only civilians would understand.

Answer: ___

14. Why does Fergusson head back into the TV sales store?

    a) He wants to buy a television.
    b) He has finished his cigarette.
    c) He does not want to look at the dead body outside.
    d) There is a customer he wants to assist.

Answer: ___

15. When did Jack Potter first see the body hanging on the lamppost?

    a) Jack Potter never sees the body hanging from the lamppost.
    b) Earlier that morning, while getting coffee.
    c) Earlier that afternoon, while getting coffee.
    d) At the same time as Ed Loyce sees it.

Answer: ___

16. Which word between lines 35 and 50 means out of control emotionally?

    a) Hysterical.

b) Hurried.

c) Pleasure.

d) Shrugged.

Answer: ___

17. Why do you think Ed Loyce whispers to himself 'I'm going nuts' at line 51.

a) Because he is the only one who can see the body hanging from the lamppost, and can't understand why nobody else can see it.

b) Because he is the only one who seems to care that a body is hanging from the lamppost, and can't understand why nobody else cares.

c) Because he is trying to cheer himself up after seeing a dead body.

d) Because he thinks he might be hallucinating.

Answer: ___

18. What type of phrase is: 'A pair of steel-rimmed glasses hung from one ear, dangling foolishly.'

a) Onomatopoeia.

b) Simile.

c) Pun.

d) Personification.

Answer: ___

19. Which of the following words taken from the passage best communicates Jenkins's irritation at being bumped into?

a) Muttered.

b) Sickened.

c) Grated.

d) Dazedly.

Answer: ___

20. What does Jenkins do for a living?

a) He works for Ed Loyce.

b) He is a police officer.

c) He is a stationery clerk.

d) He is a jeweller.

Answer: ____

21. Where does Jenkins lead Ed Loyce?

a) To the town square.

b) To the jewellery store.

c) Back to Ed Loyce's own TV shop.

d) To the Police Station.

Answer: ____

22. Which of the following phrases is a metaphor?

a) 'He stumbled and half fell'.

b) 'Women halting to see what the disturbance was'.

c) 'Loyce shouted at them frantically'.

d) 'The roar of traffic'.

Answer: ____

23. Where do you think Margaret Henderson works?

a) The Police Station.

b) The jewellery store.

c) The shoe store.

d) The Traffic Safety Council.

Answer: ____

24. Which of the following people is one of Ed Loyce's employees?

a) Packard.

b) Pete Foley.

c) Jack Potter.

d) Loyce does not have any employees.

Answer: ____

25. Why do you think the police approach Loyce at the end of the passage?

    a) Because Loyce was the one who called the police in the first place.

    b) Because they believe Loyce killed the man hanging from the lamppost.

    c) Because Loyce is reacting to the body in a way that they consider a public nuisance.

    d) Because they are trying to save Loyce from the crowd.

Answer: ___

1. Why does Ed Loyce feel tired as he heads across town?

    a) He is forty-years-old and is feeling old.
    b) He has been repairing the foundations of the house.
    c) He has been washing up.
    d) He has been working at his TV store all day.

Answer: B

This question largely hinges on retrieval, though there is some slight inference in play, too.

At line 2, we learn that Loyce 'was tired'. In the next sentence, we learn that 'his back and shoulders ached from digging dirt out of the basement and wheeling it into the back yard.' The order of those sentences leads us to infer that it is this physical labour that had induced his tiredness.

Remember, sometimes an author won't explicitly say that one thing was caused by another, or that x was because of y. Instead, we need to infer this sort of causation from how the information is presented.

Right, so we have inferred that it was the physical labour that had induced the tiredness; but crucially, at the end of the first paragraph, the narrator reveals that the physical labour Loyce had been doing had been part of 'repairing the foundations.' As a result, we know that it was this repair work that had tired Loyce out, and thus **(b)** is the correct answer.

Of all the other options, **(a)** is the one that is perhaps most likely to trip students up, since Loyce's age is mentioned shortly after we have been informed that he was feeling tired. However, we are not told that he was feeling old, nor that his age was the chief reason he was feeling tired.

2. How does Janet want to spend the money Ed Loyce has saved?

    a) On repairing the house's foundations.
    b) On purchasing a new vase.
    c) On purchasing a new TV.
    d) On purchasing a new car.

Answer: B

This is a far more straightforward retrieval question.

At lines 4-5, we are told that 'Janet could get a new vase with the money he had saved'. As a result, we know that **(b)** is the answer the examiner is looking for.

Notice that the other choices simply contain other things mentioned in the passage. The examiner is looking to ensure that the candidate is staying alert to detail and not being overly hasty.

3. What time of day is it at the start of this extract?

    a) Dawn.
    b) Midday.
    c) Midnight.
    d) Late afternoon.

Answer: D

We need to be alert to clues to land on the correct answer here.

At the start of the second paragraph, we learn 'it was getting dark' and there is mention of 'the setting sun'. This is enough information to eliminate dawn, midday, and midnight, thereby leaving us with (**d**), late afternoon.

If you missed these clues, you might have noticed instead that Loyce was looking set to arrive at his shop 'just in time to spell the help for dinner' – which again points towards the late afternoon.

4. Why do you think the author describes the commuting students as 'swarming'?

    a) Because they are moving in a way reminiscent of insects.
    b) Because it is a hot day and they are all very warm.
    c) Because the students are like parasites and sucking life out of
       the town.
    d) Because the students specialise in studying insects.

Answer: A

One could debate passionately why the author might have used the word 'swarming' here. However, this is not a debate – it is a multiple-choice paper – and so we have to identify the choice that is more likely to capture the author's intentions for this word choice.

Option (**d**) is trying to catch us out. Swarming is a word associated with the movement of insects; however, just because the students move in a way that might be described as 'swarming', this does not remotely mean they study insects – and indeed there is absolutely no indication in the passage that this is the case.

Option (**b**) is trying to catch us out in a different way. It is exploiting the fact that 'swarm' sounds like 'warm'. However, the two words have totally different meanings, so option (**b**) is not correct, either.

Now, it's not impossible that the author (as option (**c**) asserts) wants us to think of the students as parasites – after all, some insects are indeed parasites. However, to land at this conclusion, we would be taking a huge leap from a very, very slight amount of evidence… and let's not forget that it's also very possible the author *wasn't* thinking this at all by using the word 'swarming'.

On the other hand, we have option (**a**), which is asserting that the author used the word to communicate the fact the students were moving in a way reminiscent of insects. This is far less of a leap, and a much more likely and plausible answer: after all, swarming – as mentioned – is directly associated to the movement of insects. Consequently, **(a)** is the strongest answer available to us, and the one the examiner is looking for.

5. What do you think the word drab means at line 8?

    a) Business-like.
    b) Discontent and unhappy.
    c) Dreary in appearance.
    d) Angry in appearance.

Answer: C

The most common definition of drab is a dreary/dull appearance; and, if a student knows this, they will likely be able to identify **(c)** as a correct answer straight away.

Nevertheless, I would still recommend revisiting the context in which this word (or indeed any word you've been asked to define) appears, just to double check that there are no hidden tricks! However, on this occasion there are no such hidden tricks, and **(c)** is in fact the correct answer.

6. Why has Loyce driven back into town at the start of this extract?

    a) He wants to investigate what is happening in the town square.
    b) He wants to organise dinner for his employees.
    c) He wants to check in with his shop and try and make some sales.
    d) He wanted to spend some time watching the commuters.

Answer: C

At lines 10-11, as Loyce drives back into town, we learn that Loyce looked set to 'arrive just in time to spell the help for dinner, go over the records of the day, maybe even close a couple of sales himself'. From this we can infer that he was motivated to travel back into town to check on his shop and try to make some sales; therefore, **(c)** is the correct answer.

Option (**a**) is the most likely to trip students up, as investigating the situation in the town square is what Loyce winds up doing. However, this was not his reason for travelling back into town in the first place, and thus (**a**) is incorrect.

7. How does Loyce feel when he discovers there are no parking spaces outside of his shop?

    a) He is happy, because he thinks it means his shop is busy.
    b) He has no strong feelings.
    c) He feels irritated at the fact he will need to park elsewhere.
    d) He feels regretful that he stopped for so long at the traffic light.

Answer: C

We learn at lines 13-14 that, when Loyce sees there are no parking spaces outside his shop, 'He cursed under his breath and swung the car in a U-turn'. When someone curses under their breath, we might infer that they are feeling strong negative feelings. This allows us to eliminate options (**a**) and (**b**), and points us towards option (**c**).

Although Loyce may be feeling regretful about being stopped for so long at the traffic light, we are given no indication that this is the case; moreover, cursing under the breath is far more associated with irritation than regret. Therefore (**d**) it is a far weaker answer, and we can eliminate that one, too.

And thus we are left with (**c**), the answer the examiner is looking for!

8. Which of the following most accurately describes the town park?

    a) It contains a water fountain and a lamppost, but no bench.
    b) It contains a lamppost, a fountain, a bench and a dummy.
    c) It contains just a bench and a water fountain.
    d) It contains a lamppost, a fountain and a bench.

Answer: D

At lines 14-15, the reader learns that 'again [Loyce] passed the little square of green with its lonely drinking fountain and bench and single lamppost'. From this we know that there is a fountain, a bench, and a single lamppost, which allows us to eliminate (a) and (c).

We can then eliminate option (b), because although Loyce momentarily thinks the thing hanging from the lamppost is a dummy, at line 21 he realises it 'wasn't a dummy'.

Consequently, (d) is the correct answer.

9. Which phrase best describes the purpose of the first four paragraphs?

   a) To make Ed Loyce's life seem boring.
   b) To make the reader feel sorry for the man on the lamppost.
   c) To make the proceeding paragraphs seem easy to understand
       by comparison.
   d) To set the scene and introduce the presence of something
       unnerving to Ed Loyce.

Answer: D

Once again, we have one of these slightly tricky questions asking us about the purpose of a certain number of paragraphs – and again, we need to be looking for the best answer available, since (as mentioned previously) the purpose of any text can be debated fiercely, so there is (arguably) no such thing as a definitive correct answer.

There are elements of the first four paragraphs that might, in some people's opinion, make Loyce's life seem boring. However, at the end of paragraph four – which is still within the mini-passage we are being asked about – Loyce has clearly seen something very mysterious and unsettling, and this does not seem boring. Therefore, though one could argue about it, the assertion put forward by option (a) seems relatively weak.

Now, let's look at (b). It is true that we may feel sorry for the man on the lamppost. However, most of the first four paragraphs are dealing with Loyce, and it is not even revealed that the entity on the lamppost is a human until paragraph five. Moreover, the state the man's body is in is not revealed till later. So to argue that the purpose of the first four paragraphs is to induce sympathy for the man on the lamppost seems unconvincing, and (b) seems unlikely to be the answer.

Whether or not the first four paragraphs are difficult to understand is a matter of opinion. However, I do not think they are greatly more difficult to understand than the rest of the extract – and definitely not so much so that they make the paragraphs that follow seem easy by comparison. As a result, the assertion in option **(c)** is also unconvincing.

Option **(d)**, however, is fairly difficult to argue against. It is true that much of the first four paragraphs function to set the scene; and the latter portion of it does indeed introduce the presence of something that Loyce finds unnerving. As a result, **(d)** is the most convincing description of the opening four paragraph's purpose, and the answer the examiner is looking for.

10. Which is the most accurate statement regarding Ed Loyce at the end of paragraph four?

  a) **He feels indifferent about what he has seen in the town park.**
  b) **He feels guilty that he has not been at his shop all day, and eager to tell his staff about his day.**
  c) **He feels disturbed and confused by the presence in the park.**
  d) **He feels responsible for the dead body and feels scared of being caught.**

Answer: C

This question, unlike the previous one, is grounded far more in cut-and-dry conclusions we can draw from the text.

In paragraph three, Loyce is very clearly confused by what he has spotted in the park, as shown by the use of rhetorical questions: 'What the hell was it? A display of some kind?' Moreover, at the end of paragraph four, Loyce is clearly unsettled by what he can see: we are told that 'the hackles on his neck rose', a response associated with fight or flight; that he 'swallowed uneasily', the word 'uneasily' a fairly explicit reference to his frayed nerves; and that 'sweat slid out on his face and hands'.

With all this in mind, option **(c)** presents itself as the correct answer.

Moreover, we can eliminate the other choices. His fraught emotional response shows that he clearly does not feel 'indifferent' about what he has seen in the park, so **(a)** is incorrect. He has demonstrated no sense of responsibility for what he can see in the park, so **(d)** is also incorrect. Finally, at no point does he express guilt that he has not been in his shop, nor an eagerness to tell his staff about his day; accordingly, **(b)** is also incorrect.

11. What do you understand by the phrase 'gathering gloom'?

    a) Pitch darkness.
    b) Increasing darkness.
    c) Increasing mood of anxiety.
    d) Decreasing darkness.

Answer: B

The phrase 'gathering gloom' can either be used literally, to mean 'increasing darkness', or metaphorically, to convey an increasingly negative or dour mood. As a result, we can immediately eliminate options **(a)** and **(d)**.

Next, if we look at the phrase in context, we can see that it is being used literally: '"See it?" Ed pointed into the gathering gloom'. Accordingly, **(b)** is the correct answer.

12. Re-read line 30. What do you think the word 'excitedly' means in this context?

    a) Enthusiastically.
    b) Electrically.
    c) Loudly.
    d) Agitatedly.

Answer: D

We have the phrase 'in this context' appearing in this definition-style question, so we know that – even though we should *always* be looking at words in their context – it is particularly important on this occasion.

Let's look at the word as it appears at lines 29 to 31: '"How the hell long has it been there?" His voice rose excitedly. "What's wrong with everybody? They just walk on past!"'

There are a number of contexts in which 'excitedly' might mean 'enthusiastically'. However, Loyce here is clearly distressed and unnerved, and this clashes with the positive connotations associated with the word 'enthusiasm': option (a), then, is incorrect

There are rarer occasions, however, in which 'to excite' means 'to agitate', and this is just such an occasion, pointing us towards (d).

As an aside, just before the word 'excitedly', we are told that Loyce's 'voice rose excitedly'. In other words, we are already being told that Loyce is speaking increasingly loudly, whereas the word 'excitedly' is telling us the tone of these loud words – it is *not* reiterating the fact that he was speaking loudly. Hence, we can conclude with confidence that (c) is also incorrect.

13. What do you think Fergusson means by 'some sort of civic thing' at line 36?

> a) **Something educational organised by the government.**
> b) **Something that only members of the civil service would understand.**
> c) **Something that is very civilised.**
> d) **Something that only civilians would understand.**

Answer: A

Those students who know what the word 'civic' means will be at an advantage here; however, it is possible that the answer can be inferred from the context.

The word civics relates to the right and responsibilities of citizens in society. We might refer to a government programme to educate the population on one of these rights or responsibilities – say, voting – as a 'civic' programme. Likewise, we might refer to someone carrying out one of their rights or responsibilities – for instance, going to vote, or doing jury duty – as doing their 'civic' duty.

With this in mind, we can conclude that when Fergusson speculates that the body on the lamppost might be a civic thing, he is suggesting that it could be something organised by government to help educate citizens as to their rights and responsibilities. The correct answer, then, is (a).

14. Why does Fergusson head back into the TV sales store?

a) He wants to buy a television.
b) He has finished his cigarette.
c) He does not want to look at the dead body outside.
d) There is a customer he wants to assist.

Answer: D

The answer is in fact lurking at line 27, a good deal prior to when Fergusson actually heads back into the store.

When Fergusson first exits the store, he says: 'This is a big deal, Ed. I can't just leave the guy standing there'. This tells us there is a customer inside with whom Fergusson has been conversing. As a result, when Fergusson then says 'Business before pleasure' at lines 40-41 and re-enters the store, he is telegraphing that he is going back to assist this customer, and thus option (**d**) is our answer.

15. When did Jack Potter first see the body hanging on the lamppost?

a) Jack Potter never sees the body hanging from the lamppost.
b) Earlier that morning, while getting coffee.
c) Earlier that afternoon, while getting coffee.
d) At the same time as Ed Loyce sees it.

Answer: C

This is straightforward retrieval-style question.

At line 44, Potter says the following: 'Sure, Ed. I saw it this afternoon when I went out for coffee'. Ergo, (**c**) is the correct answer.

16. Which word between lines 35 and 50 means out of control emotionally?

a) Hysterical.
b) Hurried.
c) Pleasure.
d) Shrugged.

Answer: A

Immediately 'hysterical' jumps out as the probable correct answer, since to be hysterical means to be out of control of one's emotions.

However, it is wise to check the context in which it appears. Sure enough, it is used to describe Loyce just before a spell of dialogue containing a litany of exclamation marks, and which makes it clear that his emotions are increasingly frayed and heightened.

Option (**a**), then, is the correct answer.

17. Why do you think Ed Loyce whispers to himself 'I'm going nuts' at line 51.

>   a) Because he is the only one who can see the body hanging from the lamppost, and can't understand why nobody else can see it.
>   b) Because he is the only one who seems to care that a body is hanging from the lamppost, and can't understand why nobody else cares.
>   c) Because he is trying to cheer himself up after seeing a dead body.
>   d) Because he thinks he might be hallucinating.

Answer: B

In a sense, this question requires us to demonstrate to the examiner that we understand what is happening in this passage; in other words, the basic drama behind the plot.

Option (**a**) we can eliminate, as it is quite clear to the reader that others can also see the body. Similarly, we can eliminate (**d**), since other characters make it clear to Loyce personally that they too can see it. Next, we can eliminate (**c**), for Loyce is plainly not trying to cheer himself up; rather he is keen to remain in a serious mood.

This leaves us with (**b**) – the correct answer. Loyce thinks he is going 'nuts' because he is the only one who cares that there is a dead body: everyone else appears to be indifferent.

. . .

18. What type of phrase is: 'A pair of steel-rimmed glasses hung from one ear, dangling foolishly.'

a) Onomatopoeia.
b) Simile.
c) Pun.
d) Personification.

Answer: D

We can tell this is not a simile, since it does not use the words 'like' or 'as', so we can eliminate (**b**). Moreover, there is no hint of onomatopoeia, and nor is there a pun, and thus we can eliminate (**a**) and (**c**), too.

This leaves us with (**d**), personification. Notice that the glasses are described as 'dangling foolishly'. The glasses are an inanimate object, but have been given the human attribute of being foolish. This, then, is an instance of personification, meaning (**d**) is the correct answer.

19. Which of the following words taken from the passage best communicates Jenkins's irritation at being bumped into?

a) Muttered.
b) Sickened.
c) Grated.
d) Dazedly.

Answer: C

At line 64, we are told that Loyce 'bumped into a small man hurrying along the sidewalk' – we soon after discover that this is Jenkins – and then we get the following: '"Watch it!" the man grated, "Oh, it's you, Ed."'

Given that this comes immediately after Loyce bumps into Jenkins, and to be grated means to be irked, it is clear (**c**) is the answer the examiner is looking for.

As an aside, 'Muttered' – option (**a**) – is a word that could imply irritation and is probably the most likely option here to trip candidates up. However, if we locate the word in the passage (line 60), we can see that it is in fact Loyce who 'muttered', *not* Jenkins, and thus 'muttered' cannot be the correct answer.

20. What does Jenkins do for a living?

    a) He works for Ed Loyce.
    b) He is a police officer.
    c) He is a stationery clerk.
    d) He is a jeweller.

                                                      Answer: C

At line 67, shortly after Loyce bumps into Jenkins, we are told that 'the stationery clerk caught Ed's arm'. Since Jenkins is the only one with Loyce at that moment in time, we can infer that Jenkins is 'the stationery clerk', which points us to (**c**).

21. Where does Jenkins lead Ed Loyce?

    a) To the town square.
    b) To the jewellery store.
    c) Back to Ed Loyce's own TV shop.
    d) To the Police Station.

                                                      Answer: C

Again, this is a retrieval question, and requires above all an attention to detail.

At line 69, we learn that 'Jenkins led [Loyce] into the alcove of LOYCE TV SALES AND SERVICE'. This clearly indicates that (**c**) is the correct answer.

22. Which of the following phrases is a metaphor?

    a) 'He stumbled and half fell'.
    b) 'Women halting to see what the disturbance was'.
    c) 'Loyce shouted at them frantically'.
    d) 'The roar of traffic'.

Answer: D

Remember, a metaphor is an implicit comparison: a comparison that does not make itself obvious by using the word 'like' or 'as'.

The word 'roar' is used to describe the cry of a large animal. The traffic is not literally roaring; the sound it is making is implicitly being likened to an animal's cry. Therefore, option (**d**) – 'the roar of traffic' – is the metaphor.

23. Where do you think Margaret Henderson works?

    a) The Police Station.
    b) The jewellery store.
    c) The shoe store.
    d) The Traffic Safety Council

Answer: B

At line 71, we are told that 'Margaret Henderson from the jewelry store joined them'. As a result, of the options above, the most likely scenario is that Margaret Henderson works at the jewellery stores – option (**b**).

24. Which of the following people is one of Ed Loyce's employees?

    a) Packard.
    b) Pete Foley.
    c) Jack Potter.
    d) Loyce does not have any employees.

Answer: B

Ed Loyce in fact has two employees that we know about. The first is Fergusson. The second is Pete Foley. He is mentioned briefly at lines 87-88, when Loyce spots him working behind the service counter: 'Pete Foley in the back at the service counter, setting up a new Philco'. Option **(b)**, then, is the correct answer.

25. Why do you think the police approach Loyce at the end of the passage?

a) Because Loyce was the one who called the police in the first place.
b) Because they believe Loyce killed the man hanging from the lamppost.
c) Because Loyce is reacting to the body in a way that they consider a public nuisance.
d) Because they are trying to save Loyce from the crowd.

Answer: C

Again, this question is trickier, and is attempting to gauge whether the candidate has understood the events unfolding in the passage. We are never told explicitly why the police approach Loyce at the end; instead, this is something we need to infer.

The other characters throughout the passage are behaving as though Loyce is blowing things out of proportion and is behaving irrationally. It is logical to extrapolate that the police see him in the same way – in other words, that they are approaching Loyce because he is causing a public nuisance with what they perceive to be illogical behaviour. The correct answer, then, is **(c)**.

The Three-Parter Paper

In contrast to the scattershot paper, the three-parter paper separates questions into different 'types': first, you have retrieval and inference questions; next, you have definition-style questions; and third, you have questions pertaining to language techniques.

It's important to note that just because a school has structured their paper one way in one year, this does not mean they will structure it the same the following year; however, there are a number of schools that separate their questions in ways similar to this, so it's definitely a style of paper to acclimatise to.

Notice that in both the papers that follow, each question has a choice of five options as opposed to four. It is important to note, however, that three-parter papers are not significantly more likely to have questions with five options as opposed to four – indeed, you can see five-option questions in other styles of paper too (including scattershot papers!).

You will also notice that the second three-parter paper in this guide revolves around a non-fiction piece as opposed to a fiction piece. Non-fiction pieces are rarer at 11+, but they do appear from time to time, so it is definitely useful to expend some effort familiarising ourselves with such extracts!

This extract is from the start of a short story set in twentieth century New York. We join Sophie Sapinsky as she attempts to find a place to live in a predominantly Jewish neighbourhood of the city.

1   With the suitcase containing all her worldly possessions under her arm, Sophie Sapinsky elbowed her way through the noisy ghetto crowds. Pushcart peddlers and pullers-in shouted and gesticulated. Women with market-baskets pushed and shoved one another, eyes straining with the one thought—how to get the food a penny

5   cheaper. With the same strained intentness, Sophie scanned each tenement, searching for a room cheap enough for her dwindling means.

In a dingy basement window a crooked sign, in straggling, penciled letters, caught Sophie's eye: "Room to let, a bargain, cheap."

The exuberant phrasing was quite in keeping with the extravagant dilapidation of the

10   surroundings. "This is the very place," thought Sophie. "There couldn't be nothing cheaper in all New York."

At the foot of the basement steps she knocked.

"Come in!" a voice answered.

As she opened the door she saw an old man bending over a pot of potatoes on a

15   shoemaker's bench. A group of children in all degrees of rags surrounded him, greedily snatching at the potatoes he handed out.

Sophie paused for an instant, but her absorption in her own problem was too great to halt the question: "Is there a room to let?"

"Hanneh Breineh, in the back, has a room." The old man was so preoccupied filling 20   the hungry hands that he did not even look up.

Sophie groped her way to the rear hall. A gaunt-faced woman answered her inquiry with loquacious enthusiasm. "A grand room for the money. I'll let it down to you only for three dollars a month. In the whole block is no bigger bargain. I should live so."

As she talked, the woman led her through the dark hall into an airshaft room. A 25   narrow window looked out into the bottom of a chimney-like pit, where lay the accumulated refuse from a score of crowded kitchens.

"Oi weh!" gasped Sophie, throwing open the sash. "No air and no light. Outside shines the sun and here it's so dark."

"It ain't so dark. It's only a little shady. Let me only turn up the gas for you and you'll 30   quick see everything like with sunshine."

The claw-fingered flame revealed a rusty, iron cot, an inverted potato barrel that served for a table, and two soap-boxes for chairs.

Sophie felt of the cot. It sagged and flopped under her touch. "The bed has only three feet!" she exclaimed in dismay.

35   "You can't have Rockefeller's palace for three dollars a month," defended Hanneh Breineh, as she shoved one of the boxes under the legless corner of the cot. "If the bed ain't so steady, so you got good neighbors. Upstairs lives Shprintzeh Gittle, the herring-woman. You can buy by her the biggest bargains in fish, a few days older…. What she got left over from the Sabbath, she sells to the neighbors cheap…. In the 40   front lives Shmendrik, the shoemaker. I'll tell you the truth, he ain't no real shoemaker. He never yet made a pair of whole shoes in his life. He's a learner from the old country—a tzadik, a saint; but every time he sees in the street a child with torn feet, he calls in and patches them up. His own eating, the last bite from his mouth, he divides up with them."

45   "Three dollars," deliberated Sophie, scarcely hearing Hanneh Breineh's chatter. "I will never find anything cheaper. It has a door to lock and I can shut this woman out … I'll take it," she said, handing her the money.

Hanneh Breineh kissed the greasy bills gloatingly. "I'll treat you like a mother! You'll have it good by me like in your own home."

50   "Thanks—but I got no time to shmoos. I got to be alone to get my work done."

The rebuff could not penetrate Hanneh Breineh's joy over the sudden possession of three dollars.

"Long years on you! May we be to good luck to one another!" was Hanneh Breineh's blessing as she closed the door.

55   Alone in her room—*her* room, securely hers—yet with the flash of triumph, a stab of bitterness. All that was hers—so wretched and so ugly! Had her eager spirit, eager to give and give, no claim to a bit of beauty—a shred of comfort?

Perhaps her family was right in condemning her rashness. Was it worth while to give up the peace of home, the security of a regular job—suffer hunger, loneliness, and
60   want—for what? For something she knew in her heart was beyond her reach. Would her writing ever amount to enough to vindicate the uprooting of her past? Would she ever become articulate enough to express beautifully what she saw and felt? What had she, after all, but a stifling, sweatshop experience, a meager, night-school education, and this wild, blind hunger to release the dumbness that choked her?

65   Sophie spread her papers on the cot beside her. Resting her elbows on the potato barrel, she clutched her pencil with tense fingers. In the notebook before her were a hundred beginnings, essays, abstractions, outbursts of chaotic moods. She glanced through the titles: "Believe in Yourself," "The Quest of the Ideal."

Meaningless tracings on the paper, her words seemed to her now—a restless spirit
70   pawing at the air. The intensity of experience, the surge of emotion that had been hers when she wrote—where were they? The words had failed to catch the life-beat—had failed to register the passion she had poured into them.

Perhaps she was not a writer, after all. Had the years and years of night-study been in vain? Choked with discouragement, the cry broke from her, "O—God—God help
75   me! I feel—I see, but it all dies in me—dumb!"

An extract from Anzia Yezierska's 'My Own People'

PART 1

---

1. Sophie looked around with 'strained intentness' because:

    a) She was trying to read a sign in a window.
    b) She was trying to spot some cheap accommodation.
    c) She was trying to save a penny while buying food.
    d) She was trying to zone out the noisy street.
    e) She felt strained about carrying all of her valuables at once.

Answer: ___

2. The writer refers to Sophie's 'dwindling means'. By this she means that:

a) Sophie has run out of money.
b) Sophie supply of money is running short.
c) Sophie has been living well beyond her means.
d) Sophie has been living well within her means.
e) Sophie has been spending too much money on accommodation.

Answer: ___

3. The writer uses the phrase 'extravagant dilapidation' to describe the area. By this she means that:

a) Excessive money has been spent on the area.
b) The area is rundown in a way that is paradoxically almost impressive.
c) People have neglected the area.
d) Not enough money has been spent on the area's upkeep.
e) The area looks as rundown as the sign in the basement window.

Answer: ___

4. By describing the children as wearing 'all degrees of rags', the writer means that:

a) The children were wearing some very fine and beautiful rags.
b) The children were wearing rags in varying condition and of varying kind.
c) The children were wearing every type of rag it was possible to come by.
d) The children were wearing rags that were warming them up by many degrees.
e) The children were carrying rag dolls.

Answer: ___

5. The old man did not look up at Sophie because...

a) Sophie paused for too long when she entered the room.
b) He had been told by Hanneh Breineh not to.
c) He was too busy catering to dependents.
d) It was too dark to see Sophie, so there was no point.

e) He was too busy cooking the potatoes.

Answer: ____

6. Hanneh 'turn[ed] up the gas' in the room because…

a) Hanneh wanted to brag about the inverted potato barrel that served as a table.
b) Hanneh did not want Sophie to bump into the rusty cot.
c) Hanneh wanted to make sure the room was well heated.
d) Hanneh wanted to show that the flame compensated for the lack of natural light.
e) Hanneh wanted to demonstrate how easy it was to turn on the flame.

Answer: ____

7. The cot 'sagged and flopped under' Sophie's 'touch' because…

a) It was missing a leg.
b) Sophie had pressed down on it too hard.
c) It was constructed of soap boxes.
d) It was excessively damp in the room.
e) The children had broken it.

Answer: ____

8. For Hanneh, 'Rockefeller's palace' is…

a) Somewhere you can rent for just over three dollars a month.
b) A place where you are bound to have bad neighbours.
c) An example of a lavish place to live.
d) A place reserved only for royalty.
e) A place reserved only for the Rockefeller family.

Answer: ____

9. At lines 55 to 56, Sophie's 'flash of triumph' came with 'a stab of bitterness' because…

a) She felt Hanneh had treated her poorly.
b) She felt depressed at being left all alone.
c) She felt bitterly hungry, as she wasn't given any potatoes.

d) She felt the room, though hers, was small and in a horrible state.

e) She was eating something very bitter.

Answer: ___

10. What does the writer mean when she refers to Sophie's 'eager spirit, eager to give and give'?

a) She means that Sophie wishes desperately she could give more money to charity.

b) She means that Sophie has a desire to contribute to humanity artistically and emotionally.

c) She means that Sophie wants to teach others about spirituality.

d) She means that Sophie is desperate to fall in love with someone.

e) She means that Sophie is desperate to give herself over to someone in marriage.

Answer: ___

11. Sophie's family had been 'condemning her rashness' because…

a) They believed she should have organised accommodation prior to moving to New York.

b) They believed there was no value whatsoever in being a writer.

c) They felt it was dangerous for Sophie to abruptly move to New York.

d) They were uniquely judgmental people who would have condemned any of Sophie's choices.

e) She had left a stable home and a job for the sake of an unlikely dream.

Answer: ___

12. At this point of the passage, a 'wild, blind hunger' means:

a) An intense urge for food.

b) An urge to eat so much as to nearly choke.

c) An intense desire and yearning.

d) An intense lack of motivation.

e) A lack of control over inhibitions.

Answer: ___

13. The author refers to 'Meaningless tracings on the paper', which are:

a) Drawings Sophie had done in the past.
b) Words Sophie had written in the past.
c) Nonsense words Sophie had made up for a nonsense poem.
d) Words Sophie is imagining on the paper.
e) A drawing of a spirit animal with paws.

Answer: ___

14. At line 74, a 'cry broke from' Sophie because...

a) She realised she was illiterate.
b) She realised that she had never truly wanted to be a writer.
c) She was unable to read her own handwriting
d) She was intensely uncomfortable in her new apartment
e) She was unable to express herself fully through her writing.

Answer: ___

15. Considering the passage as a whole, the writer presents Sophie as:

a) A confident individual in a difficult situation.
b) Worried about money more than anything else.
c) Full of aspirations yet lacking in self-confidence.
d) Nonplussed by physical discomforts.
e) An individual willing to adapt and always optimistic.

Answer: ___

PART 2

16. What is the closest definition to the word 'loquacious'?

a) Extreme.
b) Talkative.
c) Unbridled.
d) Contemplative.
e) Moderate.

Answer: ___

17. What is the closest definition of the word 'accumulated'?

a) Amassed.
b) Broken.
c) Rotted.
d) Occasional.
e) Smelly.

Answer: ___

18. What is the closest definition of the word 'vindicate'?

a) Explain.
b) Cause.
c) Justify.
d) Disregard.
e) Prove.

Answer: ___

19. What is the closest definition of the word 'articulate'?

a) Brave.
b) Intelligent.
c) Observant.
d) Eloquent.
e) Empathetic.

Answer: ___

20. What is the closest definition of the word 'abstractions'?

a) Ideas.
b) Insults.
c) Stories.
d) Complaints.
e) Smudges.

Answer: ___

PART 3

21. Which of these lines include a metaphor?

   a) 'The claw-fingered flame revealed a rusty, iron cot'
   b) 'Hanneh Breineh kissed the greasy bills gloatingly'
   c) 'a meager, night-school education'
   d) 'she clutched her pencil with tense fingers'
   e) 'Had the years and years of night-study been in vain?'

Answer: ___

22. Which of these words is an adjective?

   a) life-beat
   b) possession
   c) straggling
   d) chaotic
   e) beautifully

Answer: ___

23. Which of these words is an adverb?

   a) Glanced.
   b) Greedily.
   c) Worldly.
   d) Quest.
   e) Meaningless.

Answer: ___

24. What types of words are these: 'herring-woman'; 'shoemaker'; 'cot; 'notebook'; 'education'.

   a) Adjectives
   b) Determiners
   c) Pronouns

d) Nouns
e) Articles

Answer: ___

25. What word could be used to describe 'but' in this quote: 'Sophie paused for an instant, but her absorption in her own problem was too great to halt the question.'

a) Precursor
b) Pronoun
c) Adverb
d) Appendage
e) Conjunction

Answer: ___

PART 1

1. Sophie looked around with 'strained intentness' because…

    a) She was trying to read a sign in a window.
    b) She was trying to spot some cheap accommodation.
    c) She was trying to save a penny while buying food.
    d) She was trying to zone out the noisy street.
    e) She felt strained about carrying all of her valuables at once.

Answer: B

This is a different style of question to any we've encountered thus far – one in which we are required to finish the sentence, following on from the word 'because'. However, in many respects, it is testing very similar skills to the 'Why…?' questions we saw in the previous paper.

Also, notice how this time round we have five options as opposed to four. But don't worry too much: because while a fifth option may make life that little bit more tricky, we can still use the same tactics we used when confronted with just the four options.

Now, back to the question…

It may sound obvious, but when a 'complete the sentence' style question includes a quote from the extract, always be sure to re-read the section in which that quote appears. Here, for instance, is where the phrase 'strained intentness' appears: 'With the same strained intentness, Sophie scanned each tenement, searching for a room cheap enough for her dwindling means'.

We can see, then, that Sophie is looking with strained intentness in an attempt to find a cheap room. Option (**b**), it follows, is the correct answer.

Remember, though, that sometimes you will need to read the sentences that appear either side of the sentence in which the quote appears to find the answer. That said, notice that many of the incorrect options take or adapt phrases that appear in sentences near to where the correct answer is lurking. The examiner is making sure that we are paying attention: take your time and read carefully!

2. The writer refers to Sophie's 'dwindling means'. By this she means that:

    a) Sophie has run out of money.
    b) Sophie supply of money is running short.
    c) Sophie has been living well beyond her means.
    d) Sophie has been living well within her means.
    e) Sophie has been spending too much money on accommodation.

Answer: B

This question is also asking us to finish a sentence. However, in many respects it is simply another definition style question: it is asking us to give the meaning of a particular phrase.

However, this is a trickier question than it might at first seem, because there are options here that might trip us up. Let's take a closer look at where the difficulties lie.

The correct answer here is (**b**). A person's means refers to the money and assets they have in their possession; and if something is dwindling, it means that it is decreasing or running out.

However, an option like (**c**) could trip some candidates up because, if someone's means are dwindling, it would be reasonable to infer that they are living beyond their means. But remember: we are looking for the best answer of the bunch. Option **(c)** might well be an accurate explanation of *why* Sophie's means are dwindling, but option **(b)** is still the most accurate definition of what the phrase means.

Option **(e)** is very similar to **(c)**. Given that Sophie is looking for a cheap place to live, it is very possible that Sophie's means have been dwindling because she had previously been spending too much on accommodation. Yet while this might be true, **(b)** remains a more accurate definition of the phrase 'dwindling means'.

Finally, we know that Sophie has not run out of money altogether – after all, she pays Hanneh for the room! – so **(a)** can also be eliminated.

3. The writer uses the phrase 'extravagant dilapidation' to describe the area. By this she means that:

    a) **Excessive money has been spent on the area.**
    b) **The area is rundown in a way that is paradoxically almost impressive.**
    c) **People have neglected the area.**
    d) **Not enough money has been spent on the area's upkeep.**
    e) **The area looks as rundown as the sign in the basement window.**

Answer: B

Again, we have a question asking us to define a phrase. And again, it is tricky because there are options here designed to trip candidates up.

The phrase 'extravagant dilapidation' is an oxymoron. This is when two words which have the opposite meaning are placed together. The phrase 'loving hate' from Shakespeare's *Romeo and Juliet* is a famous example of an oxymoron. The word 'love' has the opposite meaning to 'hate', yet they are being placed side by side.

The word 'extravagant' refers to over-the-top spending and luxury, whereas dilapidation refers to a state of extreme disrepair and neglect. Putting the words together in the way the author has paradoxically implies that the dilapidation of the area is so extreme as to almost be impressively over-the-top. Option **(b)**, therefore, is the correct answer.

Of the other options, **(c)** and **(d)** are most likely to trip students up. Given that the area is extremely dilapidated, it is reasonable to infer both that people have neglected the area and that not enough money has been spent on its upkeep. However, while these statements may well both be true, **(b)** remains the best answer available – the one that most accurately defines the phrase in question.

4. By describing the children as wearing 'all degrees of rags', the writer means that:

   a) **The children were wearing some very fine and beautiful rags.**
   b) **The children were wearing rags in varying condition and of varying kind.**
   c) **The children were wearing every type of rag it was possible to come by.**
   d) **The children were wearing rags that were warming them up by many degrees.**
   e) **The children were carrying rag dolls.**

Answer: B

For the third time on the trot, we are being asked to demonstrate our understanding of a particular phrase.

The phrase 'all degrees' here means something akin to 'all kinds' – in other words, the author is referring to lots of different kinds of rags, and in lots of different conditions. The best fit, then, is option **(b)**.

I'd imagine option **(c)** is the one most likely to trip students up. In the same way the phrase 'all kinds' does not mean 'every kind', the word 'all' in 'all degrees' does not mean 'every'. As a result, the author is *not* trying to say that the children are wearing every type of rag that you could possibly come by.

5. The old man did not look up at Sophie because...

   a) **Sophie paused for too long when she entered the room.**
   b) **He had been told by Hanneh Breineh not to.**
   c) **He was too busy catering to dependents.**
   d) **It was too dark to see Sophie, so there was no point.**
   e) **He was too busy cooking the potatoes.**

Answer: C

Notice we have another "complete the sentence" style question hinging on the word 'because'. As mentioned already, questions of this kind can easily be reformulated into 'Why...?' style questions similar to those we saw in previous papers. 'Why did the old man not look up at Sophie?'

Above all, we being tested here on our retrieval skills.

At lines 19-20 we learn that 'The old man was so preoccupied filling the hungry hands that he did not even look up'. This tells us that **(c)** is the correct answer: he was too busy ('preoccupied') handing out food to the dependents/children ('hungry hands') to look up.

6. Hanneh 'turn[ed] up the gas' in the room because...

    a) **Hanneh wanted to brag about the inverted potato barrel that served as a table.**
    b) **Hanneh did not want Sophie to bump into the rusty cot.**
    c) **Hanneh wanted to make sure the room was well heated.**
    d) **Hanneh wanted to show that the flame compensated for the lack of natural light.**
    e) **Hanneh wanted to demonstrate how easy it was to turn on the flame.**

Answer: D

At lines 27-28, Sophie complains about the lack of natural light in the room: she says 'Outside shines the sun and here it's so dark'. In response to this, Hanneh turns on the gas-powered flame to show Sophie that it compensates for the meagre sunlight: 'Let me only turn up the gas for you and you'll quick see everything like with sunshine'. Option **(d)**, then, is the correct answer.

As an aside, it is possible that Hanneh also wanted to demonstrate how easy it was to turn on the flame, as option **(e)** suggests, or did not want Sophie to bump into the cot, as **(b)** suggests. However, the extract does not tell us any of this explicitly – we would be projecting motives onto Hanneh that we are not certain she has – and thus these options are far weaker than **(d)** (and would, in consequence, not get you the mark!).

· · ·

7. The cot 'sagged and flopped under' Sophie's 'touch' because...

    a) It was missing a leg.
    b) Sophie had pressed down on it too hard.
    c) It was constructed of soap boxes.
    d) It was excessively damp in the room.
    e) The children had broken it.

Answer: A

At lines 33-34, after we learn that the cot 'sagged and flopped under her touch', Sophie says the following: 'The bed has only three feet'. Ergo: option **(a)** is the correct answer.

Some candidates might be wary that Sophie could, with the word 'feet', be referring to the length or width of the bed (after all, a foot is also a unit to measure distance); however, notice that at line 36 there is mention of the cot's 'legless corner', which confirms that the cot was missing a foot/leg.

8. For Hanneh, 'Rockefeller's palace' is...

    a) Somewhere you can rent for just over three dollars a month.
    b) A place where you are bound to have bad neighbours.
    c) An example of a lavish place to live.
    d) A place reserved only for royalty.
    e) A place reserved only for the Rockefeller family.

Answer: C

This is a more subtle question: it is trying to gauge whether we understand how Hanneh uses her reference to 'Rockefeller's palace'.

First, let's take a look at the context in which it appears. It appears at line 35, and is spoken by Hanneh in response to Sophie complaining about the condition of the room:

'"You can't have Rockefeller's palace for three dollars a month," defended Hanneh Breineh, as she shoved one of the boxes under the legless corner of the cot.'

Even though students might not know who Rockefeller was (he was one of the wealthiest people in modern history!), the word palace should be enough to tell candidates that Hanneh is referring to a luxurious and expensive building. She is, in effect, telling Sophie that she cannot expect the height of luxury for just $3 dollars a month – and thus she is using Rockefeller's palace as a symbol of such luxury, an example of a lavish home that one should not expect at such a humble price.

Option (**c**), then, is the correct answer.

Some students – especially those who don't recognise the name Rockefeller – might have gone with (**d**) instead: after all, the word 'palace' is often used to refer to royal residences. However, Rockefeller was *not* a royal, and thus (**d**) is an example of the examiners being a bit mean and intentionally throwing in a plausible-seeming (yet still ultimately incorrect!) option.

9. At lines 55-56, Sophie's 'flash of triumph' came with 'a stab of bitterness' because...

    a) She felt Hanneh had treated her poorly.
    b) She felt depressed at being left all alone.
    c) She felt bitterly hungry, as she wasn't given any potatoes.
    d) She felt the room, though hers, was small and in a horrible state.
    e) She was eating something very bitter.

Answer: D

Let's take a look at the section of the extract from which this question is drawing its quotes: 'Alone in her room—*her* room, securely hers—yet with the flash of triumph, a stab of bitterness. All that was hers—so wretched and so ugly!'

Reading this carefully, we can see that the triumph is derived from having her own room, whereas the bitterness is coming from it being in a 'wretched' and 'ugly' state. This pairs nicely with option (**d**) above.

10. What does the writer mean when she refers to Sophie's 'eager spirit, eager to give and give'?

    a) **She means that Sophie wishes desperately she could give more money to charity.**
    b) **She means that Sophie has a desire to contribute to humanity artistically and emotionally.**
    c) **She means that Sophie wants to teach others about spirituality.**
    d) **She means that Sophie is desperate to fall in love with someone.**
    e) **She means that Sophie is desperate to give herself over to someone in marriage.**

Answer: B

We are not told explicitly what it is that Sophie (and her 'eager spirit') feels 'eager to give' in this extract; so we need to pick the option above that best tallies with what we can infer from the passage.

We know that Sophie is an aspiring writer, so it seems reasonable to conclude that what she wants to 'give' to the world and humanity is her art and thoughts. This tallies with option (**b**).

However, given that the answer is requiring inference, it is wise to eliminate the other options, just to ensure none of the other answers are somehow more convincing.

Option (**a**) asserts the phrase suggests Sophie wishes desperately she had more money, so she would have excess to give to others. However, there is no mention in this passage of giving charity, or any mention that Sophie wishes to earn more money (let alone pass it on), and so (**a**) is a weaker answer.

Insofar as option (**c**) is concerned, there is no mention at all that Sophie is interested in spirituality, or that she wishes to teach others about spirituality. In other words, option (**c**) is trying to trip up those candidates who might have misinterpreted the phrase 'eager spirit' as indicating that Sophie has a heartfelt interest in spirituality or wishes to teach the subject.

Options (**d**) and (**e**) propose, in slightly different ways, that Sophie wishes to give herself in a romantic sense. However, there is absolutely no evidence of any desire to pursue romantic interests, or get married, in this extract. Options (**d**) and (**e**), then, are also weak choices.

Having gone through all the other choices, (**b**) continues to stand head and shoulders above the rest as the most reasonable inference, and is indeed the choice the examiner is looking for.

· · ·

11. Sophie's family had been 'condemning her rashness' because…

    a) They believed she should have organised accommodation prior to moving to New York.

    b) They believed there was no value whatsoever in being a writer.

    c) They felt it was dangerous for Sophie to abruptly move to New York.

    d) They were uniquely judgmental people who would have condemned any of Sophie's choices.

    e) She had left a stable home and a job for the sake of an unlikely dream.

Answer: E

As ever, let's revisit the context in which this quote appears:

'Perhaps her family was right in condemning her rashness. Was it worth while to give up the peace of home, the security of a regular job—suffer hunger, loneliness, and want—for what? For something she knew in her heart was beyond her reach.'

In the two sentences just after the mention of her family condemning her rashness, there is mention that Sophie had given up 'peace of home' and 'the security of a regular job', and that she had done so to try and achieve something that was 'beyond her reach'. Given how these sentences are structured, we are pointed firmly in the direction of option (**e**): that her family had been condemning the rashness of giving up a stable home and job for the sake of a dream.

12. At this point of the passage, a 'wild, blind hunger' means:

    a) An intense urge for food.

    b) An urge to eat so much as to nearly choke.

    c) An intense desire and yearning.

    d) An intense lack of motivation.

    e) A lack of control over inhibitions.

Answer: C

At lines 62-64, the reader is confronted with the following rhetorical question about Sophie's life: 'What had she, after all, but a stifling, sweatshop experience, a meager, night-school education, and this wild, blind hunger to release the dumbness that choked her?'

The hunger, then, is not a literal one, but a metaphorical one – Sophie has a desire and yearning (a metaphorical hunger) to express herself and conquer 'the dumbness that choked her'. As such, option (c) is the correct answer.

13. The author refers to 'Meaningless tracings on the paper', which are...

    a) Drawings Sophie had done in the past.
    b) Words Sophie had written in the past.
    c) Nonsense words Sophie had made up for a nonsense poem.
    d) Words Sophie is imagining on the paper.
    e) A drawing of a spirit animal with paws.

Answer: B

This quote is drawn from the following sentence: 'Meaningless tracings on the paper, her words seemed to her now—a restless spirit pawing at the air'.

We are being told that, although they seem to Sophie like 'meaningless tracings on the paper', they are in fact 'words' that have been written there. This allows us to whittle down our potential answers to options (b) and (c).

Option (c) is, in fact, trying to trip us up: the words are not 'meaningless' to Sophie because they are nonsense words, but because she has lost confidence in the quality of her writing. Option (b), then, is the correct answer.

As an aside, the reference to 'a restless spirit pawing at the air' in the quote I've included above is in fact a metaphor: it is likening the words Sophie had written to just such a 'restless spirit'. As a result, there is no literal drawing of a 'restless spirit' – option (e) is designed to trip up those candidates who do not realise that this image is metaphorical.

14. At line 74, a 'cry broke from' Sophie because…

a) **She realised she was illiterate.**
b) **She realised that she had never truly wanted to be a writer.**
c) **She was unable to read her own handwriting**
d) **She was intensely uncomfortable in her new apartment**
e) **She was unable to express herself fully through her writing.**

Answer: E

The answer is lurking in the extract's final paragraph:

'Perhaps she was not a writer, after all. Had the years and years of night-study been in vain? Choked with discouragement, the cry broke from her, "O—God—God help me! I feel—I see, but it all dies in me—dumb!"'

To be dumb is to be unable to speak. Sophie, with this final comment, is suggesting that she feels that she is unable to fully express herself in her writing – that she feels, when she writes, as though she has been rendered dumb. Accordingly, option **(e)** is the correct answer.

15. Considering the passage as a whole, the writer presents Sophie as:

a) **A confident individual in a difficult situation.**
b) **Worried about money more than anything else.**
c) **Full of aspirations yet lacking in self-confidence.**
d) **Nonplussed by physical discomforts.**
e) **An individual willing to adapt and always optimistic.**

Answer: C

The final question of this section of the paper is trying to gauge the candidate's total understanding of the extract. When faced with a question asking us about multiple paragraphs at once – or, indeed, the entire extract – I'd suggest that the process of elimination is the best way forward.

Option **(a)** suggests Sophie is a confident individual; however, this clearly clashes with her self-doubts about her writing skills, and thus clearly ought to be eliminated. In a similar vein, option **(e)** describes Sophie as optimistic, yet she is in fact deeply pessimistic throughout the passage about her ability to succeed as a writer – so this option, too, ought to be eliminated.

Earlier we saw that Sophie had a 'stab of bitterness' about the miserable state of her new room. Option **(d)** is suggesting that Sophie is 'nonplussed' (in other words, uncaring and un-fussed) about physical discomforts, but this is clearly not true, and is thus another option we can eliminate.

While it does appear that Sophie is concerned about money, it seems a stretch to suggest (as option **(b)** does) that she is concerned about it 'more than anything else'. In fact, she also seems deeply concerned about her writing career, as well as her family.

This leaves us with **(c)**. Certainly, Sophie is full of aspirations: she clearly wants to be a writer. It is also true that she lacks self-confidence in her writing abilities: she sees her words as being as valueless as 'meaningless tracings'. Option **(c)**, then, is the correct answer.

PART 2

16. What is the closest definition to the word 'loquacious'?

  a) **Extreme.**
  b) **Talkative.**
  c) **Unbridled.**
  d) **Contemplative.**
  e) **Moderate.**

Answer: B

The second section of this paper is dedicated exclusively to single word definitions. As ever, even if you think you know the definition, it is wise to re-read the context in which the word appears, if only to double check that your chosen answer fits!

Moreover, if you are unsure of the answer, it can be useful to swap the original word in with each of the various choices you've been given in order to see which one seems to fit best. This is not guaranteed to work, but it at least lets you make an educated guess.

The correct answer to this particular question is **(b)**: Hanneh is being described as talkative.

17. What is the closest definition of the word 'accumulated'?

a) Amassed.
b) Broken.
c) Rotted.
d) Occasional.
e) Smelly.

Answer: A

To accumulate means to amass or to build up over a period of time, hence **(a)** is the answer.

In other words, the window in Sophie's room looks out at a pile of rubbish which has been thrown out by the other kitchens in the apartment block and which has built up over time!

18. What is the closest definition of the word 'vindicate'?

a) Explain.
b) Cause.
c) Justify.
d) Disregard.
e) Prove.

Answer: C

To be vindicated can mean either to be absolved of guilt, or to be shown to be justified. On this occasion, it is the latter meaning the author is using: Hanneh wants to justify her decision to uproot her past life by succeeding as a writer. Option **(c)**, then, is correct.

19. What is the closest definition of the word 'articulate'?

a) **Brave.**
b) **Intelligent.**
c) **Observant.**
d) **Eloquent.**
e) **Empathetic.**

Answer: D

The word 'articulate' can be both an adjective and a verb, and in this extract it appears as an adjective: 'Would she ever become articulate enough to express beautifully what she saw and felt?'

When used as an adjective, articulate means something akin to eloquent: it refers to the ability to make oneself understood clearly. Option (**d**), then, is correct.

As an aside, 'articulate', when used as a verb, means something akin to 'communicate'. To articulate your thoughts is to communicate them.

20. What is the closest definition of the word 'abstractions'?

a) **Ideas.**
b) **Insults.**
c) **Stories.**
d) **Complaints.**
e) **Smudges.**

Answer: A

The word abstraction means something similar to idea or concept, so (**a**) is the correct answer.

PART 3

21. Which of these lines include a metaphor?

    a) 'The claw-fingered flame revealed a rusty, iron cot'
    b) 'Hanneh Breineh kissed the greasy bills gloatingly'
    c) 'a meager, night-school education'
    d) 'she clutched her pencil with tense fingers'
    e) 'Had the years and years of night-study been in vain?'

Answer: A

Remember, a metaphor is when you have an implicit comparison: a comparison that does not make use of 'like' or 'as'.

The expression 'claw-fingered flame' is likening the flame to fingers with claws, but this comparison is not made explicit through the use of the word 'like' or 'as'. Accordingly, (**a**) is correct.

22. Which of these words is an adjective?

    a) Life-beat.
    b) Possession.
    c) Straggling.
    d) Chaotic.
    e) Beautifully.

Answer: D

An adjective is a descriptive word: more specifically, it is descriptive word used to describe a noun.

It's important to look at each word as it appears in context, as certain words might be an adjective in one context, but not in others.

The correct answer here is (**d**). In the phrase 'chaotic moods', the word 'moods' is a noun, and the word 'chaotic' is the adjective that describes the noun: it is telling us what kind of moods.

A noun, by the way, is a word that refers to an individual, a place, a thing, an idea, an event, a state of being, or a quality.

. . .

23. Which of these words is an adverb?

   a) Glanced.
   b) Greedily.
   c) Worldly.
   d) Quest.
   e) Meaningless.

                                     Answer: B

An adverb is a type of describing word that is used to describe *not* a noun, but a verb, adjective or phrase. They often end with the letters 'ly', though remember: not all adverbs end with 'ly', and not all words that end with 'ly' are adverbs.

Again, it is profoundly important to look at the words in context in order to figure out whether they are adverbs.

The correct answer above is (**b**), 'greedily'. Let's look at the sentence within which it appears: 'A group of children in all degrees of rags surrounded him, greedily snatching at the potatoes he handed out'. The word 'greedily' here is describing the word 'snatching', which is a verb (a doing word). As a result, we know it is an adverb.

Notice that option (**c**), 'worldly', is a word that ends in 'ly'. However, it has been placed there to trip us up, as it is actually an adjective. It appears at the very start of the extract, in the phrase 'all her worldly possessions'. Since 'worldly' is describing 'possessions' – a noun – we know it is an adjective, not an adverb.

24. What types of words are these: 'herring-woman'; 'shoemaker'; 'cot; 'notebook'; 'education'.

   a) Adjectives.
   b) Determiners.
   c) Pronouns.
   d) Nouns.
   e) Articles.

                                     Answer: D

These words are all nouns, hence option **(d)** is correct.

We know that these are not describing words, so we can eliminate **(a)**.

A determiner is a word that appears before a noun and which informs us of a quantity. So, for example, in the phrase 'eight potatoes', the word 'eight' is the determiner. As such, we can eliminate **(b)**.

A pronoun is a word that substitutes in for a noun in certain contexts. Examples would be 'he', 'she', 'they', 'him', 'she', 'them', and so on. Option **(c)**, then, can also be eliminated.

In grammar, an article helps us understand whether a noun is specific or not. So when the word 'the' appears before a noun — for instance, 'the laptop' — the word 'the' is the article, and it is telling us that a specific laptop is being referred to. An indefinite article, on the other hand, would be the word 'a' in the phrase 'a laptop': the word 'a' is the article, and it is telling us that we are *not* dealing with a specific laptop. However, since none of these words in the question above are articles, we can eliminate option **(e)** as well.

25. What word could be used to describe 'but' in this quote: 'Sophie paused for an instant, but her absorption in her own problem was too great to halt the question'.

    a) Precursor.
    b) Pronoun.
    c) Adverb.
    d) Appendage.
    e) Conjunction.

Answer: E

A conjunction is a word that is used to connect words, phrases, clauses or sentences. Examples include 'but', 'and', 'because', 'so', 'whether' and 'yet'. As such, **(e)** is the correct answer.

The word precursor is in fact simply there to trip us up, and is not a word that relates to grammar. It refers to when an event comes before a second event – the first event is the precursor. Ergo, **(a)** is incorrect.

We have looked at the definitions of pronouns and adverbs, and we know that the word 'but' here is neither of these, thus **(b)** and **(c)** are also incorrect.

The word 'appendage' is another non-grammatical word that has been included to throw us off! It simply refers to an object or a thing that is affixed or attached to something larger. Option **(e)**, then, is also incorrect.

Paper Four: A Description of Quebec
THREE-PARTER PAPER; DEVILISH; 45 MINUTES

This is a non-fiction description of Quebec, Canada, written by the English writer, William Bingley, who visited the city in the late nineteenth century.

1   This city, the capital of Canada, stands at the northern extremity of a strip of high land, which follows the course of the river St. Lawrence, as far as the mouth of the Charles. The basis of these heights is a dark slate rock, of which most of the build-ings in the town are constructed. *Cape Diamond* terminates the promontory, with a
5   bold precipice towards the river. This rock derives its name from numerous trans-parent crystals, which are found upon it; and which are so abundant that, after a shower of rain, the ground glitters with them.

The Lower Town of Quebec is built at the foot of the heights; and the Upper Town occupies their crest. The former, snug and dirty, is the abode of persons engaged in
10   trade, and of most of the lower classes: the latter, lofty and cold, is the seat of govern-ment, and the principal residence of the military.

With few exceptions, the *houses* in Quebec are built of stone. The roofs of the better sort are covered with sheets of iron or tin, and those of an inferior description, with boards. On the roofs ladders are usually placed, near the garret-windows, for the
15   purpose of the chimney-sweepers ascending, on the outside, to clean the chimneys: for, in this country boys do not go up the chimneys, as in England; but two men, one at the top and the other at the bottom, sweep them, by pulling up and down a bundle of twigs or furze, tied to a rope.

The *streets* of the Lower Town are, for the most part, narrow and irregular. St. Peter's
20   street is the best paved, and the widest of the whole. It contains several good and
substantial *houses*, which are chiefly occupied by merchants and traders; but, from the
colour of the stone of which the houses are constructed, and of the iron roofs, all the
streets of Quebec have a heavy and gloomy appearance.

A street, called *Mountain Street*, which leads to the Upper Town, winds, in a serpentine
25   direction, from the market-place up the hill, and terminates near the Upper Town
market-place. This street, in winter, is extremely dangerous. The quantity of snow
and ice, which here accumulate in large masses, renders it necessary for the inhabitants to wear outer shoes, that are shod with iron spikes. The boys of Quebec have a
favourite amusement, in lying at full length with their breast upon a small kind of
30   sledge, and sliding along the snow, from the top of the hill to the bottom: they glide
down with astonishing velocity; yet, with their feet, they can guide or stop themselves,
at pleasure.

The *shops* or stores of the traders in the Lower Town, do not exhibit any of that
diversified and pleasing appearance which is so remarkable in London. Here the
35   stranger sees nothing but heavy stone buildings, gloomy casements, and iron-cased
shutters, painted red. If any show is made at the window, it is with paltry articles of
cooking, earthen and hardware: there is, however, a tolerable display of bear-skins,
seal-skins, foxes-tails, and buffalo-robes.

The *taverns* in Quebec are numerous; yet a stranger is much surprised to find only two
40   houses which deserve that high-sounding appellation. This arises from the vanity that
possesses all our trans-Atlantic brethren, to designate their paltry public-houses or
spirit-shops, by the more dignified title of "tavern;" for through the whole of America, every dirty hole, where a few glasses of rum, gin, or whisky, are sold, is so called.

The *markets* of Quebec are well supplied with every thing that the country affords;
45   and, in general, at a very cheap rate. In the autumn, as soon as the river betwixt the
town and the island of Orleans, is frozen over, an abundance of provisions is received
from that island. The Canadians, at the commencement of winter, kill the greatest
part of their stock, and carry it to market in a frozen state. The inhabitants of the
towns supply themselves, at this season, with butcher's meat, poultry, and vegetables,
50   to serve them till spring. These are kept in garrets or cellars; and, so long as they
continue frozen, their goodness is preserved. Before they are prepared for the table,
they are laid for some hours in cold water, to be thawed. In wintertime, milk is
brought to market in large frozen cakes.

An extract adapted from William Bingley's 'Travels in North America'

PART 1

1. The phrase 'terminates the promontory' in line 4 suggests that:

a) *Cape Diamond* is at the very end of the promontory.
b) *Cape Diamond* is where Charles has been killed.
c) *Cape Diamond* is another term for a promontory.
d) *Cape Diamond* has been mined to source building materials.
e) *Cape Diamond* is considered a symbol of death.

Answer: ____

2. In lines 4 to 7, the writer tells us:

a) *Cape Diamond* is covered in diamonds.
b) *Cape Diamond* is the location of a promenade.
c) *Cape Diamond* experiences abundant rainfall.
d) *Cape Diamond* is named after the glittering crystals found there.
e) *Cape Diamond* is famous for being mostly transparent.

Answer: ____

3. Lines 8 to 11 tell us that:

a) The town's crest features an image of the Upper Town.
b) The less wealthy people generally live in the Lower Town.
c) The military are in the Upper Town so they can see approaching enemies.
d) The 'lower class' people are called this because they live lower down.
e) The Upper Town can only be reached by foot.

Answer: ____

4. In lines 10 to 11, the phrase 'the seat of government' refers to the fact that:

a) The government's buildings are located in this area.
b) Members of government make speeches while sitting.
c) Members of government relax in this area.
d) The government has deep-seated biases.
e) The area elects people to sit in parliament.

Answer: ____

5. In lines 14 to 18 we are told that in Quebec they clean chimneys by:

a) Placing ladders inside the chimney for cleaners to climb.
b) Sending English boys up the chimney.
c) Entering by a special garret-window.
d) Having two individuals at either end use a sweeping device.
e) Attaching bundles of twigs or furze to the roof.

Answer: ____

6. In lines 19 to 23 the writer describes St Peter's Street as:

a) The least narrow in the Lower Town.
b) Exclusively occupied by merchants and traders.
c) The heaviest and gloomiest street in the Lower Town.
d) The only street in Lower Town with high quality paving.
e) A moving tribute to Saint Peter.

Answer: ____

7. Lines 24 to 32 tell you that Mountain Street is a street that:

a) People must always wear iron spiked shoes to walk along.
b) Is constructed on a hill.
c) Is infested with snakes.
d) Carriages ride along at astonishing velocity.
e) Terminates in the middle of the Upper Town's market-place.

Answer: ____

8. The phrase 'at pleasure' in line 32 suggests that:

a) The children take pleasure in the sledging.
b) The children enjoy using their feet while sledging.
c) The children can use their feet at will to control their sledging.
d) The writer finds it pleasurable to watch the children sledging.
e) The name of the slope is known as "pleasure".

Answer: ____

9. Lines 33 to 36 tell us that:

a) The shops in the Lower Town are less attractive than those in the Upper Town.
b) Shop owners in England are more ethnically diverse than those in Quebec.
c) Some of the shops in the Lower Town display newspaper articles.
d) The shops in the Lower Town are less interesting visually than those in England.
e) It is the law that all the shops are painted red in the Lower Town.

Answer: ____

10. In line 37 the word 'tolerable' suggests that:

a) The display of animal products is just about acceptably eye-catching.
b) The writer tolerates people cruelly killing animals to make products.
c) The writer does not tolerate the display of animal-derived products.
d) The writer must pay a toll to view this display.
e) The display of animal products is insufficiently eye-catching.

Answer: ____

11. In line 40, the writer refers to the word 'tavern' as 'a high-sounding appellation'. Does he mean:

a) The label "tavern" is used when a building seems to be higher up than it truly is.
b) The label "tavern" is used only in the height of summer.
c) The label "tavern" implies a building that is high above sea level.
d) The label "tavern" implies grandeur and gravitas.
e) The label "tavern" is an unappealing one.

Answer: ____

12. The 'trans-Atlantic brethren' referred to in line 41 are:

a) People living on the American continents.
b) People living on the European continent.
c) The writer's family members who live in Quebec.
d) People living in Quebec who are related to people living in England.
e) People who travel frequently across the Atlantic Ocean.

Answer: ___

13. Quebec receives produce from the island of Orleans only once Autumn arrives because:

a) Orleans harvests all its food produce in Autumn and no sooner.
b) The commute can only be made once the river between the towns has frozen.
c) Religious ceremonies prevent trade from taking place sooner.
d) The produce must be transported in a frozen state during colder months.
e) There is only demand in the run up to Christmas.

Answer: ___

14. During the winter, food in Quebec is 'laid for some hours in cold water' before it is served at the table because:

a) The cold water is filled with salt, which preserves the food.
b) It has been kept in the cellars and garrets for so long.
c) It is compulsory according to something called the thaw law.
d) This ensures the food is clean.
e) This allows the food to slowly defrost.

Answer: ___

15. Considering the passage as a whole, the writer presents Quebec as:

a) A city far more glamourous and beautiful than London.
b) A village in an exceptionally cold climate.
c) A city comprised of two parts and built on an incline.
d) A city torn apart by inequality.
e) A very interesting town that is also the capital of the United States.

Answer: ___

PART 2

16. What is the closest definition to the word 'extremity'?

a) Hill.
b) Slice.
c) Side.
d) Limit.
e) Valley.

Answer: ___

17. What is the closest definition to the word 'abundance'?

a) Quantity.
b) Assortment.
c) Profusion.
d) Ship-full.
e) Delectable.

Answer: ___

18. What is the closest definition to the word 'designate?

a) Parody.
b) Deride.
c) Dignify.
d) Foment.
e) Classify.

Answer: ___

19. What is the closest definition to the word 'abode'?

a) Workplace.
b) Hideout.
c) Home.
d) Abbot.
e) Bank.

Answer: ___

20. What is the closest definition to the word 'vanity'?

a) Egotism.
b) Delusion.

c) Frivolity.
d) Solemnity.
e) Superstition.

Answer: ___

PART 3

---

21. What types of words are these: 'glitters'; 'occupies'; 'accumulate'; 'renders'; 'supplied'.

a) Adjectives.
b) Verbs.
c) Prefixes.
d) Nouns.
e) Adverbs.

Answer: ___

22. Which of these lines include a metaphor?

a) 'Here the stranger sees nothing but heavy stone buildings'
b) 'winds, in a serpentine direction, from the market-place up the hill'
c) 'with their feet, they can guide or stop themselves'
d) 'sweep them, by pulling up and down a bundle of twigs or furze'
e) 'The boys of Quebec have a favourite amusement'

Answer: ___

23. Which of these words as they are used in the extract is a verb?

a) Buildings.
b) High-sounding.
c) Winds.
d) Astonishing.
e) Pleasing.

Answer: ___

24. Which of these words from the extract is an adverb?

a) Stone.
b) Terminates.
c) Lying.
d) Usually.
e) Supply.

Answer: ___

25. Which of these words from the extract is an adjective?

a) Velocity.
b) Lofty.
c) Thawed.
d) Articles.
e) Purpose.

Answer: ___

PART 1

1. The phrase 'terminates the promontory' in line 4 suggests that:

    a) *Cape Diamond* **is at the very end of the promontory.**
    b) *Cape Diamond* **is where Charles has been killed.**
    c) *Cape Diamond* **is another term for a promontory.**
    d) *Cape Diamond* **has been mined to source building materials.**
    e) *Cape Diamond* **is considered a symbol of death.**

Answer: A

This is another "complete the sentence" style question – on this occasion, we are being asked to tease out the implications of a certain phrase.

The termination point of something is its end point: we might say that a train terminates at its final stop. A promontory is a piece of land that extends out into the sea. Thus, the correct answer is **(a)**: the writer is saying that *Cape Diamond* is at the very end of the promontory.

· · ·

2. In lines 4 to 7, the writer tells us:

a) *Cape Diamond* is covered in diamonds.
b) *Cape Diamond* is the location of a promenade.
c) *Cape Diamond* experiences abundant rainfall.
d) *Cape Diamond* is named after the glittering crystals found there.
e) *Cape Diamond* is famous for being mostly transparent.

Answer: D

This is a slightly different style of question to any we have faced thus far, but the skills required should now be familiar enough. The name of the game is to re-read the section of the passage specified, glean from the section what the writer is trying to relay, and match it up with the correct answer. It is all about showing an understanding of the content.

The incorrect options will often say something that is similar to what is being said in the extract, yet subtly different in a way that makes it technically incorrect; so we need to be paying attention.

The correct answer here is **(d)**. At lines 5-6, we are told the following: 'This rock derives its name from numerous transparent crystals, which are found upon it'. This clearly states that *Cape Diamond* gets its name from the crystals to be found there.

Let's take a quick look at one of the options trying to catch us out. Option **(c)** claims that *Cape Diamond* experiences abundant rainfall. However, while the writer does use the word 'abundant' in the sentence discussing the impact of rainfall on *Cape Diamond*, he is using it to describe the quantity of crystals, and *not* the rainfall itself.

So long as we are working carefully, there is no reason to be caught out by something like this; but we need to be vigilant!

3. Lines 8 to 11 tell us that:

a) The town's crest features an image of the Upper Town.
b) The less wealthy people generally live in the Lower Town.
c) The military are in the Upper Town so they can see approaching enemies.
d) The 'lower class' people are called this because they live lower down.

e) The Upper Town can only be reached by foot.

Answer: B

The correct answer here is (**b**): we are told that 'the former' – a reference to the Lower Town, as mentioned in the previous sentence – is the 'abode' (home) of 'most of the lower classes' (and members of the lower classes will generally be less wealthy).

4. In lines 10-11, the phrase 'the seat of government' refers to the fact that:

    a) The government's buildings are located in this area.
    b) Members of government make speeches while sitting.
    c) Members of government relax in this area.
    d) The government has deep-seated biases.
    e) The area elects people to sit in parliament.

Answer: A

The seat of government is an expression used to describe a location where the government and its buildings are based, and thus (**a**) is the correct answer.

5. In lines 14 to 18 we are told that in Quebec they clean chimneys by:

    a) Placing ladders inside the chimney for cleaners to climb.
    b) Sending English boys up the chimney.
    c) Entering by a special garret-window.
    d) Having two individuals at either end use a sweeping device.
    e) Attaching bundles of twigs or furze to the roof.

Answer: D

The answer to this is lurking at lines 16-18, where we have the following information: 'two men, one at the top and the other at the bottom, sweep them [the chimneys], by pulling up and down a bundle of twigs or furze, tied to a rope'. Consequently, **(d)** is the correct answer.

Again, let's take a look at one of the options attempting to catch us out. Option **(b)** asserts that they clean the chimneys by 'sending English boys up'. However, while boys and England are mentioned in this section of the passage, it is explicitly mentioned that this is *not* how the chimneys in Quebec are cleaned: 'in this country boys do not go up the chimneys, as in England'. This option is looking to catch out those candidates not paying attention to details.

6. In lines 19 to 23 the writer describes St Peter's Street as:

   a) The least narrow in the Lower Town.
   b) Exclusively occupied by merchants and traders.
   c) The heaviest and gloomiest street in the Lower Town.
   d) The only street in Lower Town with high quality paving.
   e) A moving tribute to Saint Peter.

Answer: A

At lines 19-20 we are told that 'St Peter's street is the best paved, and the widest of the whole'. If it is the widest street in the Lower Town, it logically follows that it is also the least narrow; therefore, **(a)** is the correct answer.

Again, let's take a look at one of the other options trying to mislead us. Option **(b)** is asserting that St Peter's Street is 'exclusively' occupied by 'merchants and traders'. However, this is subtly incorrect, as in fact it is 'chiefly' (that is, mostly) occupied by merchants and traders, but not exclusively so. As a result, option **(b)** is incorrect.

7. Lines 24 to 32 tell you that Mountain Street is a street that:

   a) People must always wear iron spiked shoes to walk along.
   b) Is constructed on a hill.
   c) Is infested with snakes.
   d) Carriages ride along at astonishing velocity.
   e) Terminates in the middle of the Upper Town's market-place.

Answer: B

We are told that Mountain Street winds 'from the market-place up the hill'; in other words, it is constructed on a hill, so **(b)** is correct.

Notice how option **(e)** suggests that Mountain Street terminates in the middle of the Upper Town market place. This is another attempt to catch us out. Mountain Street in fact terminates 'near' the Upper Town's market place, not in the middle of it.

8. The phrase 'at pleasure' in line 32 suggests that:

    a) **The children take pleasure in the sledging.**
    b) **The children enjoy using their feet while sledging.**
    c) **The children can use their feet at will to control their sledging.**
    d) **The writer finds it pleasurable to watch the children sledging.**
    e) **The name of the slope is known as "pleasure".**

Answer: C

The phrase 'at pleasure' means 'at will'. For example, if I was riding on a horse, and was able to make the horse go faster or slower whenever I wanted, I could say that I was able to control the horse's pace at pleasure. In light of this, we know that **(c)** is the correct answer.

Option **(a)** might attract candidates who are unfamiliar with the phrase; however, to do something 'at pleasure' does not mean that someone is having a pleasurable time while doing said thing.

9. Lines 33 to 36 tell us that:

    a) **The shops in the Lower Town are less attractive than those in the Upper Town.**
    b) **Shop owners in England are more ethnically diverse than those in Quebec.**
    c) **Some of the shops in the Lower Town display newspaper articles.**
    d) **The shops in the Lower Town are less interesting visually than those in England.**

e) It is the law that all the shops are painted red in the Lower Town.

Answer: D

At lines 33-34, the writer asserts that the shops of Lower Town 'do not exhibit any of that diversified and pleasing appearance which is so remarkable in London'. In other words, the shops are not so visually pleasing or varied in Quebec as they are in London, hence (**d**) is the correct answer.

As an aside, the word 'diversified' here means varied. We can see that option (**b**) is trying to catch out those candidates who thought it might be referring to ethnic diversity!

10. In line 37 the word 'tolerable' suggests that:

a) The display of animal products is just about acceptably eye-catching.

b) The writer tolerates people cruelly killing animals to make products.

c) The writer does not tolerate the display of animal-derived products.

d) The writer must pay a toll to view this display.

e) The display of animal products is insufficiently eye-catching.

Answer: A

Although 'tolerable' can mean something like 'endurable' or 'bearable', it can also mean something slightly more positive, such as 'adequate' or 'acceptable'. It is the latter usage of the word 'tolerable' the writer is using here – he is saying that the display in these Quebec shop window is adequately/acceptably eye-catching – and thus (**a**) is the correct answer.

11. In line 40, the writer refers to the word 'tavern' as 'a high-sounding appellation'. Does he mean:

a) **The label "tavern" is used when a building seems to be higher up than it truly is.**

b) **The label "tavern" is used only in the height of summer.**

c) **The label "tavern" implies a building that is high above sea level.**

d) **The label "tavern" implies grandeur and gravitas.**

e) **The label "tavern" is an unappealing one.**

Answer: D

The word 'appellation' means name. The phrase 'high-sounding' means something along the lines of 'important sounding' or 'grand sounding'. Ergo: the writer is saying that the word 'tavern' implies somewhere important or grand: option (**d**), then, is correct.

12. The 'trans-Atlantic brethren' referred to in line 41 are:

a) **People living on the American continents.**

b) **People living on the European continent.**

c) **The writer's family members who live in Quebec.**

d) **People living in Quebec who are related to people living in England.**

e) **People who travel frequently across the Atlantic Ocean.**

Answer: A

The word 'brethren' means 'brother', but can also really be used to refer to a whole group of people someone feels fondly about. For instance, if you really get along well with everyone at your school – girls and boys alike – you could refer to them as your brethren.

The phrase trans-Atlantic is an interesting one. When used by people from the Americas, it refers to Europeans: the people on the other side of the Atlantic. Conversely, when used by people from Europe, it refers to people in the Americas – again, the people on the other side of the Atlantic. Since this writer is English and is writing about Canadians – a country just north of the United States – we know that he is referring to people in the Americas when he uses the phrase 'trans-Atlantic brethren'; and so (**a**) is the correct answer.

As an aside, we know that the writer is from England not from the passage, but the snippet of text just before the passage. Always remember to read the entirety of what you've been given – and that includes the text introducing the extract – because there are occasions when this might be pivotal to identifying the correct answer!

13. Quebec receives produce from the island of Orleans only once Autumn arrives because:

    a) Orleans harvests all its food produce in Autumn and no sooner.

    b) The commute can only be made once the river between the towns has frozen.

    c) Religious ceremonies prevent trade from taking place sooner.

    d) The produce must be transported in a frozen state during colder months.

    e) There is only demand in the run up to Christmas.

                                                   Answer: B

At lines 45-47 we learn that 'In the autumn, as soon as the river betwixt the town and the island of Orleans, is frozen over, an abundance of provisions is received from that island'. From this we can infer that trade between the town of Quebec and the island of Orleans does not take place prior to Autumn because the river between ('betwixt') these locations is *not* frozen over.

Accordingly, **(b)** is the correct answer.

14. During the winter, food in Quebec is 'laid for some hours in cold water' before it is served at the table because:

    a) The cold water is filled with salt, which preserves the food.

    b) It has been kept in the cellars and garrets for so long.

    c) It is compulsory according to something called the thaw law.

    d) This ensures the food is clean.

    e) This allows the food to slowly defrost.

                                                   Answer: E

The second last sentence of the passage reads as follows: 'Before they are prepared for the table, they are laid for some hours in cold water, to be thawed'.

The word 'thawed' is a synonym of 'defrosted': the food is place in the cold water to allow it to defrost. Option **(e)**, then, is correct.

15. Considering the passage as a whole, the writer presents Quebec as:

    a) **A city far more glamourous and beautiful than London.**
    b) **A village in an exceptionally cold climate.**
    c) **A city comprised of two parts and built on an incline.**
    d) **A city torn apart by inequality.**
    e) **A very interesting town that is also the capital of the United States.**

Answer: C

We are being asked to comment on the contents of the passage as a whole. As mentioned already, the process of elimination is our best bet with this style of question.

London is mentioned just once in this passage – at line 34 – where it is referenced as a city with more attractive and beautiful shops than those in Quebec. As such, option **(a)** is patently incorrect.

Quebec is presented as having an exceptionally cold climate: there is mention of winter sports and we are told how the river ices over. However, Quebec is crucially *not* a village, but a city, as mentioned in the passage's opening sentence, meaning **(b)**, too, is incorrect.

Option **(c)** describes the city as being comprised of two parts and being built on an incline (a hill/mountain). Sure enough, at lines 8-9, we are told of the two constituent parts of Quebec, and the fact it is built on a slope: 'The Lower Town of Quebec is built at the foot of the heights; and the Upper Town occupies their crest'. Option **(c)** looks to be a strong, credible answer.

The city does appear to be divided on the basis of wealth: the 'lower classes', we are told, live for the most part in the Lower Town, and the elites in the Upper Town. However, while there is indeed inequality, there is no indication – as **(d)** asserts – that the city is 'torn apart' (a phrase that implies acrimony and anger) as a result of this inequality. Option **(d)**, then, is weaker than **(c)**.

Finally, the assertion in option **(e)** that Quebec is the capital of America is contradicted in the passage's opening sentence, where we are told that it is in fact 'the capital of Canada'.

Our best answer – and the one the examiner is looking for – is **(c)**.

PART 2

16. What is the closest definition to the word 'extremity'?

    a) Hill.
    b) Slice.
    c) Side.
    d) Limit.
    e) Valley.

Answer: D

As in the previous paper, the second section of this paper is dedicated to definitions of individual words as they appear in the passage.

At line 1, we have the following expression: 'the northern extremity of a strip of high land'. The extremity of something is its limit or endpoint. Therefore, **(d)** is correct.

17. What is the closest definition to the word 'abundance'?

    a) Quantity.
    b) Assortment.
    c) Profusion.
    d) Ship-full.
    e) Delectable.

Answer: C

At line 46 there is mention of 'an abundance of provisions'. An abundance means 'lots of' or 'a profusion', so **(c)** is the correct answer.

18. What is the closest definition to the word 'designate?

a) **Parody.**
b) **Deride.**
c) **Dignify.**
d) **Foment.**
e) **Classify.**

Answer: E

When used as a verb – as it is in this passage (see line 41) – 'designate' can either mean to appoint an individual to a position, or to give someone or something a certain name or classification.

The writer is using the second of these meanings and, as such, **(e)** is the best option of the choices above.

19. What is the closest definition to the word 'abode'?

a) **Workplace.**
b) **Hideout.**
c) **Home.**
d) **Abbot.**
e) **Bank.**

Answer: C

'Abode' is another word 'home', so **(c)** is correct.

20. What is the closest definition to the word 'vanity'?

a) **Egotism.**
b) **Delusion.**

c) **Frivolity.**
d) **Solemnity.**
e) **Superstition.**

Answer: A

To be vain is to be self-important or egotistical; that is, to have a high opinion of oneself. As such, (**a**) is the correct answer.

PART 3

21. What types of words are these: 'glitters'; 'occupies'; 'accumulate'; 'renders'; 'supplied'.

a) **Adjectives.**
b) **Verbs.**
c) **Prefixes.**
d) **Nouns.**
e) **Adverbs.**

Answer: B

These are all 'doing' words, and thus they are all verbs (option (**b**)).

22. Which of these lines include a metaphor?

a) **'Here the stranger sees nothing but heavy stone buildings'**
b) **'winds, in a serpentine direction, from the market-place up the hill'**
c) **'with their feet, they can guide or stop themselves'**
d) **'sweep them, by pulling up and down a bundle of twigs or furze'**
e) **'The boys of Quebec have a favourite amusement'**

Answer: B

The phase 'serpentine direction' in option **(b)** implicitly likens the winding of the road to the shape of a snake/the way a snake moves (serpentine is a word that relates to snakes). Since the comparison is implicit and does not make use of 'like' or 'as', we know it is a metaphor.

23. Which of these words as they are used in the extract is a verb?

     a) **Buildings.**
     b) **High-sounding.**
     c) **Winds.**
     d) **Astonishing.**
     e) **Pleasing.**

Answer: C

Students are often told that words ending with 'ing' are usually verbs. This particular question has intentionally given us four options ending in 'ing', yet none of them happen to be verbs. Indeed, it is **(c)**, 'winds', that is the verb among this selection!

Remember: don't just assume a word falls into a certain category just because it ends with a particular set of letters. Yes, looking at the way a word is spelt can offer clues, but never just go by this alone!

24. Which of these words from the extract is an adverb?

     a) **Stone.**
     b) **Terminates.**
     c) **Lying.**
     d) **Usually.**
     e) **Supply.**

Answer: D

Let's look at the phrase in which 'usually' appears: 'roofs ladders are usually placed…'

'Placed' is a verb, and 'usually' is used to describe that verb. As a result, 'usually' is an adverb, so (d) is the correct answer.

25. Which of these words from the extract is an adjective?

    a) Velocity.
    b) Lofty.
    c) Thawed.
    d) Articles.
    e) Purpose.

Answer: B

Remember: an adjective is a descriptive word used to describe a noun.

The correct answer is 'lofty', which means something along the lines of 'imposingly high up'. It is being used in this extract to describe Quebec's 'Upper Town'. Option (b), then, is correct.

The Poetry Paper

The poetry paper stands out not because of how the questions are organised (indeed, they are usually organised in a way reminiscent of scattershot papers), but because the text the candidate needs to interact with is a poem instead of a piece of prose.

I would say that poetry comprehension papers are a good deal rarer than prose papers. That said, some schools do favour them. And, at the risk of sounding like a broken record, do keep in mind that schools are liable to change their style of paper from year to year – I have seen certain schools who have historically favoured prose comprehensions shift to poetry without warning – and we want to be prepared for all eventualities.

Generally speaking, poetry papers tend to have fewer questions in total than prose papers, if only because poems are usually shorter than prose pieces. This is nothing to stress about; it's just another quirk to be aware of.

Finally, a quick note about poetry itself. Many students find the thought of engaging with a poem intimidating. My advice is to keep a cool head, read through the text multiple times, and to accept that there might be words or phrases that the poet has intentionally made difficult – or even impossible – to fully understand. My other advice is to always be asking yourself: does the poet mean this literally or metaphorically?

Paper Five: The Donkey
POETRY PAPER; DIFFICULT; 30 MINUTES

1   When fishes flew and forests walked
    And figs grew upon thorn,
    Some moment when the moon was blood
    Then surely I was born;

5   With monstrous head and sickening cry
    And ears like errant wings,
    The devil's walking parody
    On all four-footed things.

    The tattered outlaw of the earth,
10 Of ancient crooked will;
    Starve, scourge, deride me: I am dumb,
    I keep my secret still.

    Fools! For I also had my hour;
    One far fierce hour and sweet:
15 There was a shout about my ears,
    And palms before my feet.

G.K. Chesterton's 'The Donkey'

1. Who is the speaker in this poem?

    a) The owner of a donkey.
    b) The devil.
    c) The donkey.
    d) An omniscient narrator.

Answer: ___

2. In lines 3-4, why does the poet write that the donkey was 'born' during 'some moment when the moon was blood'?

    a) The poet is conveying that someone was murdered when the donkey was born.
    b) The poet is conveying that there was pollution when the donkey was born.
    c) The poet is emphasising how the donkey sees himself as unnatural and aberrant.
    d) The poet is telling us that the donkey's mother died giving birth.

Answer: ___

3. Why does the poet describe the donkey's ears as being 'like errant wings' in line 6?

    a) The donkey is able to fly.
    b) The donkey's ears make him look like an angel.
    c) The donkey's ears make him look like he can fly, even though he cannot.
    d) The donkey's ears are absurd in size and shape.

Answer: ___

4. Why is the apostrophe used in line 7: 'The devil's walking parody'?

    a) It is short for 'devil is'.
    b) To suggest the donkey is the devil's creation.
    c) It is a typographical mistake.
    d) It is short for 'devil was'.

Answer: ___

5. What does 'parody' mean in line 7?

a) Parody means that the donkey is a ridiculous-seeming imitation of other animals.

b) Parody means that the donkey is lacking in intellect.

c) Parody sounds like rhapsody and means pet.

d) Parody is the sound a donkey makes, in the same way as a horse is said to neigh.

Answer: ___

6. Line 11 uses a punctuation mark to individualise the items in a list. What is the mark called?

a) Semi-colon.

b) Brackets.

c) Comma.

d) Ellipsis.

Answer: ___

7. 'I am dumb, / I keep my secret still.' Which are the verbs in this sentence?

a) 'am' and 'keep'

b) 'dumb' and 'secret'

c) 'I' and 'I'

d) 'am' and 'still'

Answer: ___

8. Why do you think the poet has the donkey use the word 'Fools' at line 13?

a) The donkey is referring to his entire species as foolish.

b) The donkey is pushing back against those who misunderstood and belittled him.

c) The donkey is jokingly referring to the people reading the poem as fools.

d) The donkey is rebuking the devil and his minions.

Answer: ___

9. Line 11 uses a technique in which two words start with the same letter. How do you spell this technique?

a) Alliteration
b) Aliteration
c) Alitteration
d) Allitteration

Answer: ____

10. What do you understand the phrase in line 16 'palms before my feet' to mean?

a) People had laid palm tree leaves at the donkey's feet.
b) People had tried to stop the donkey from moving with their hands.
c) People had bowed down before the donkey in praise.
d) The donkey used to have palms, but they have been transformed into feet.

Answer: ____

1. Who is the speaker in this poem?

 a) **The owner of a donkey.**
 b) **The devil.**
 c) **The donkey.**
 d) **An omniscient narrator.**

Answer: C

The correct answer here is (**c**): the speaker is the donkey.

You are more likely to be asked to identify the speaker in a poem, since it can often be trickier to work out.

There are a number of clues that point us towards it being (**c**), the donkey. Let's look at a few of them.

First, we have the title. While this does not guarantee anything, it primes us to expect that the donkey is likely to be the speaker.

Second, notice at line 8 how the speaker refers to himself as a 'four-footed' thing. This points us towards (**c**), and definitely eliminates (**a**), since we'd assume a donkey's owner to be human (and thus two-footed).

Third, there is the mention of the speaker's 'monstrous head' and 'sickening cry', which strongly implies a donkey; after all, donkeys are known for the distinctive shape of their heads and their cries. Moreover, this encourages us to eliminate **(a)** and **(d)**, as these are not attributes we would expect of a human owner, nor an omniscient (all knowing) narrator.

Fourth, the phrase 'The devil's walking parody' encourages us to eliminate **(b)**: the speaker seems to be saying that he belongs to, or was created by, the devil, and *not* that he is the devil himself.

Moreover, notice that the speaker of the poem often uses the phrase 'I'. Usually, an omniscient narrator talks about other characters, not themselves, so the fact we have the word 'I' used suggests again that **(d)** is incorrect.

Collectively, all of this (and in fact there is further evidence in the poem!) points us towards the fact that the donkey is the speaker and thus **(c)** is correct.

2. In lines 3-4, why does the poet write that the donkey was 'born' during 'some moment when the moon was blood'?

    a) **The poet is conveying that someone was murdered when the donkey was born.**
    b) **The poet is conveying that there was pollution when the donkey was born.**
    c) **The poet is emphasising how the donkey sees himself as unnatural and aberrant.**
    d) **The poet is telling us that the donkey's mother died giving birth.**

Answer: C

The correct answer here is **(c)**. Let's explore how we know this is the case.

We describe a paragraph of a poem as a stanza. Here's the poem's opening stanza:

> When fishes flew and forests walked
> And figs grew upon thorn,
> Some moment when the moon was blood
> Then surely I was born;

At line three we have the mention of 'when the moon was blood'. However, it is not the only way the poet describes the moment when the donkey was born: it was also when 'fishes flew' and 'forests walked' and 'figs grew upon thorn'. Collectively, what do these images tell us? What do they have in common?

The idea of fishes flying is an unnatural thought: fishes don't fly, they swim. The idea of forests walking is similarly unnatural: the trees, after all, are rooted to the ground. Indeed, the image of figs growing from thorns is just as unnatural again: the thorns protect the fruit – they are not where the fruit actually emanates from.

The image of the moon being blood, then, should not be taken in isolation. Rather, it is linked to these other images of unnaturalness, which encourages us to see it in this same light. Indeed, sure enough, when we examine the image, we see that it too is an image that evokes unnaturalness: we think of the moon as being white or a luminescent yellow, *not* blood red.

However, the poet is not suggesting that these things were literally happening when the donkey was born. Rather, they are *metaphors* for the donkey's own unnaturalness; the donkey's own aberrant nature. As such, (c) is the answer the examiner is looking for.

3. Why does the poet describe the donkey's ears as being 'like errant wings' in line 6?

a) **The donkey is able to fly.**
b) **The donkey's ears make him look like an angel.**
c) **The donkey's ears make him look like he can fly, even though he cannot.**
d) **The donkey's ears are absurd in size and shape.**

Answer: D

The correct answer here is (**d**).

Again, we do not want to look at this image in isolation. It comes just after the poet has had the donkey describe his own 'monstrous head' and 'sickening cry'. It appears, then, that the donkey is discussing his own hideousness when he uses this simile likening his ears to 'errant wings'. Indeed, the word 'errant' means out of bound or out of proportion, and 'wings' suggest that they are large in relation to his body, and thus the donkey is saying that his ears look hideously and absurdly large.

· · ·

4. Why is the apostrophe used in line 7: 'The devil's walking parody'?

    a) It is short for 'devil is'.
    b) To suggest the donkey is the devil's creation.
    c) It is a typographical mistake.
    d) It is short for 'devil was'.

Answer: B

We have in fact already revealed the answer to this in our explanation to question one: this line suggests that the donkey belongs to the devil or is the devil's creation. Option (**b**), then, is the correct answer.

In short, this question is trying to discern whether candidates understand the difference between apostrophes used to connote ownership, and apostrophes used to combine two words.

5. What does 'parody' mean in line 7?

    a) Parody means that the donkey is a ridiculous-seeming imitation of other animals.
    b) Parody means that the donkey is lacking in intellect.
    c) Parody sounds like rhapsody and means pet.
    d) Parody is the sound a donkey makes, in the same way as a horse is said to neigh.

Answer: A

You will notice that in some papers, when we are asked to define a single word, we are merely given a list of single words and need to pick a synonym. However, this question is doing things slightly differently and offering longer definitions.

The reason for this difference in style is due to the fact that many individual schools create their own 11+ papers in-house, and so they will often have attributes that are unique to that school's exam papers. This is not something to panic about, but it is definitely something to be aware of.

A parody is a mocking imitation of something. If you were to do an impression of your teacher, but emphasised some of their mannerisms to make them seem ridiculous, you would be parodying them.

The donkey is describing himself in just this way – as a ridiculous imitation of other four-footed animals – meaning option (**a**) is correct.

6. Line 11 uses a punctuation mark to individualise the items in a list. What is the mark called?

a) **Semi-colon.**
b) **Brackets.**
c) **Comma.**
d) **Ellipsis.**

Answer: C

Let's take a look at line 11 in its entirety: 'Starve, scourge, deride me: I am dumb'

There are in fact just two punctuation marks used here: you have the commas, which separate the list of abuses the donkey faces, and then the colon after the word 'me'.

Since we do not have the choice of a colon in the list of options above, we know that the answer must be (**c**) – though this is also clear, given that the commas are indeed individualizing items in this line.

Colons, as an aside, are used to introduce a list or to expand on a thought. In this instance, the poet is using it as a means to expand upon a thought.

Semi colons are the commas with a dot hovering above them: ";". They can also be used to individualize the items in a list – though they are usually only used when each item in the list takes multiple words to describe. They are also used as an alternative to a conjunction to connect two linked clauses. On this occasion, no semi-colons are present, so (**a**) is incorrect.

Brackets are used to insert a clause or add an extra thought (and, when used, look like this). These are not present anywhere in the poem, so (**b**) is incorrect.

An ellipsis is when you have three dots in a row, like this: '…' They are used to communicate a sense of open-endedness or incompletion. They are not present in line 11, however, and thus (**d**) is incorrect.

. . .

7. 'I am dumb, / I keep my secret still.' Which are the verbs in this sentence?

  a) 'am' and 'keep'
  b) 'dumb' and 'secret'
  c) 'I' and 'I'
  d) 'am' and 'still'

Answer: A

Verbs are doing words. 'Keep' is a doing word, and that points us immediately towards **(a)** – the correct answer. Moreover, 'am' is a doing word, too – in fact, perhaps the most fundamental of the doing words!

8. Why do you think the poet has the donkey use the word 'Fools' at line 13?

  a) **The donkey is referring to his entire species as foolish.**
  b) **The donkey is pushing back against those who misunderstood and belittled him.**
  c) **The donkey is jokingly referring to the people reading the poem as fools.**
  d) **The donkey is rebuking the devil and his minions.**

Answer: B

Option **(b)** here is the correct answer.

In the penultimate (second to last) stanza, just before the word 'Fools' appears, we see the donkey addressing those people who abuse and belittle him, almost seeming to encourage them: 'Starve, scourge, deride me'. When the word 'Fools' then appears, it therefore follows that the donkey is in fact still addressing those people: he is turning the tables on them and pointing to their stupidity for having abused him.

9. Line 11 uses a technique in which two words start with the same letter. How do you spell this technique?

a) **Alliteration**
b) **Aliteration**
c) **Alitteration**
d) **Allitteration**

Answer: A

This is in fact a spelling question; and this is certainly a good word for any 11+ candidate to learn to spell. Remember, the double letter in alliteration is on the 'l', not the 't'.

10. What do you understand the phrase in line 16 'palms before my feet' to mean?

a) **People had laid palm tree leaves at the donkey's feet.**
b) **People had tried to stop the donkey from moving with their hands.**
c) **People had bowed down before the donkey in praise.**
d) **The donkey used to have palms, but they have been transformed into feet.**

Answer: C

The correct answer is **(c)**: people had bowed down to the donkey.

A clue that something positive is happening is the line just beforehand that tells us this event happened during 'one far fierce hour and sweet'. The idea that this hour was 'sweet' implies extreme joy, and this at the very least eliminates option **(b)**, which seems to be quite a negative scenario. Indeed, there is no evidence whatsoever that the people had tried to stop the donkey from moving, further casting **(b)** as an incorrect choice.

The idea that there was 'a shout about [the donkey's] ears' suggests that there are people around him and interacting with him. As a result, it seems likely that the 'palms before [his] feet' belong to these same people, and are not the donkey's own. This, combined with the fact that there is no evidence whatsoever that the donkey had his palms transformed to feet, suggest that option **(d)** should also be eliminated.

Option **(a)** feels fairly positive, and suggests that the 'palms' are not the donkeys own. However, there is no evidence that 'palms' refer to palm leaves as opposed to people's palms. Given this lack of evidence, option **(c)** outdoes **(a)** as the most likely scenario, and thus is the best answer available to us.

As an aside, this poem is in fact built on a biblical reference. In the bible, as Jesus arrived in Jerusalem on a donkey, the crowd praised and bowed before him. The donkey in this poem appears to be the same donkey Jesus rode, and the 'fierce hour' seems to refer to this incident. As demonstrated above, we don't need to know this reference to work out the answer – but it allows us to see with even greater certainty that **(c)** is correct.

Paper Six: The Apology
POETRY PAPER; DEVILISH; 30 MINUTES

1   Think me not unkind and rude,
     That I walk alone in grove and glen;
     I go to the god of the wood
     To fetch his word to men.

5   Tax not my sloth that I
     Fold my arms beside the brook;
     Each cloud that floated in the sky
     Writes a letter in my book.

     Chide me not, laborious band,
10   For the idle flowers I brought;
     Every aster in my hand
     Goes home loaded with a thought.

     There was never mystery,
     But 'tis figured in the flowers,
15   Was never secret history,
     But birds tell it in the bowers.

     One harvest from thy field
     Homeward brought the oxen strong;
     A second crop thine acres yield,
20   Which I gather in a song.

Ralph Waldo Emerson's The Apology

---

1. At lines 3-4 to poet writes: 'I go to the god of the wood/ To fetch his word to men.' What do you understand this to mean?

   a) The poet receives enlightenment by spending time in nature.

   b) The poet hallucinates that he met a deity in the woods who spoke to him.

   c) The poet encounters a noble animal, who he considers the god of the woods.

   d) The poet considers himself the god of the wood.

Answer: ___

2. Why does the poet say that each 'cloud' 'writes a letter in' his 'book'?

   a) Because the poet uses rainwater to help make the ink with which he writes.

   b) Because the cloud imparts wisdom that inspires the poet to write.

   c) Because the poet is more likely to write in his book on a rainy day.

   d) Because a friend of the poet's, who lives beyond the horizon, writes him letters.

Answer: ___

3. What does 'sloth' mean in this context?

   a) Sloth refers to an animal, which happens to be the poet's pet.

   b) Sloth suggests that the poet's behaviour might be seen as lazy.

   c) Sloth means the money the poet makes.

   d) Sloth sounds like cloth and refers to the poet's clothes.

Answer: ___

4. At lines 6 to 7 the poet writes: 'Chide me not, laborious hand, / For the idle flowers I brought.' Which are the verbs in these lines?

   a) 'Chide' and 'laborious'

   b) 'laborious' and 'idle'

   c) 'idle' and 'chide'

   d) 'Chide' and 'brought'

Answer: ___

5. An aster is a type of flower. Why does the poet describe 'every' aster as 'loaded with a thought'?

   a) Because each flower has been loaded into the poet's arms.
   b) Because the poet is thinking about picking loads more flowers.
   c) Because the flower inspires philosophical contemplations in the poet.
   d) Because the poet is likening the flower to a gun.

Answer: ___

6. Why is the apostrophe used in line 14: 'But 'tis figured in the flowers'?

   a) It is a typographical mistake.
   b) To suggest the figure belongs to the flowers.
   c) It is short for 'it is'.
   d) It is short for 'it was'.

Answer: ___

7. What is it that the poet is suggesting the birds 'tell in their bowers'?

   a) The fact that history is an illusion.
   b) The secret that all of history has taken place only in that forest.
   c) Wisdom akin to a kind of secret history.
   d) The song that the poet then sings at the end of the poem.

Answer: ___

8. Halfway through every sentence is a punctuation mark. What is this mark called?

   a) Colon.
   b) Semi-colon.
   c) Comma.
   d) Ellipsis.

Answer: ___

9. Why do you think the poet describes the 'acres' as yielding a 'second crop'?

a) The second crop refers to the wisdom the poet receives from the land.
b) The acres are incredibly fertile so can produce two crops in one year.
c) These are simply the lyrics to the song the poet is singing.
d) The second crop refers to the food the poet will eat himself.

Answer: ___

10. The first and third line in every stanza rhymes, and so too do the second and fourth line. How do you spell this technique?

a) Alternate Ryme
b) Alternate Ryme
c) Allternate Rhyme
d) Alternate Rhyme

Answer: ___

1. At lines 3-4 to poet writes: 'I go to the god of the wood/ To fetch his word to men.' What do you understand this to mean?

    a) The poet receives enlightenment by spending time in nature.
    b) The poet hallucinates that he met a deity in the woods who spoke to him.
    c) The poet encounters a noble animal, who he considers the god of the woods.
    d) The poet considers himself the god of the wood.

Answer: A

The correct answer here is (**a**).

The poet here is not speaking literally – he is not seeking out a literal god who will communicate literal words. Rather, he metaphorically sees nature as a kind of divine, godly entity, and construes spending time in nature as educational: as metaphorically akin to receiving godly words of wisdom.

Always be pondering whether the poet is writing literally or metaphorically. This is an area that multiple choice poetry papers frequently like to quiz candidates on, but also a concern that is essential to understanding poetry in general!

. . .

2. Why does the poet say that each 'cloud' 'writes a letter in' his 'book'?

   a) Because the poet uses rainwater to help make the ink with
      which he writes.
   b) Because the cloud imparts wisdom that inspires the poet to
      write.
   c) Because the poet is more likely to write in his book on a
      rainy day.
   d) Because a friend of the poet's, who lives beyond the horizon,
      writes him letters.

Answer: B

The answer here is (**b**).

Again, the writer is talking metaphorically. The cloud does not literally write in his book, nor does the poet literally use the rain from a cloud in order to create the ink with which he writes, as option (**a**) suggests. Rather, he is saying that the cloud imparts a certain kind of wisdom that inspires him to write in his book.

3. What does 'sloth' mean in this context?

   a) Sloth refers to an animal, which happens to be the poet's pet.
   b) Sloth suggests that the poet's behaviour might be seen as lazy.
   c) Sloth means the money the poet makes.
   d) Sloth sounds like cloth and refers to the poet's clothes.

Answer: B

A sloth is indeed a type of animal; however, it is can also be used as another word for lazy or idle.

When the poet writes 'tax not my sloth', he is using the second meaning of the word. As a result, option (**b**) is correct: he is saying that his behaviour could be construed as lazy.

. . .

4. At lines 6 to 7 the poet writes: 'Chide me not, laborious hand, / For the idle flowers I brought.' Which are the verbs in these lines?

a) 'Chide' and 'laborious'
b) 'laborious' and 'idle'
c) 'idle' and 'chide'
d) 'Chide' and 'brought'

Answer: D

The two verbs here are 'chide' – which means something like 'to tell off' or 'reprimand' – and 'brought'. Ergo: **(d)** is the correct answer.

5. An aster is a type of flower. Why does the poet describe 'every' aster as 'loaded with a thought'?

a) Because each flower has been loaded into the poet's arms.
b) Because the poet is thinking about picking loads more flowers.
c) Because the flower inspires philosophical contemplations in the poet.
d) Because the poet is likening the flower to a gun.

Answer: C

The poet here is continuing to communicate his belief that natural phenomena contain, and have the ability to impart, a kind of wisdom. As such, option **(c)** is the best answer, here: the 'thought' that is 'loaded' in the 'aster' is, in fact, a kind of divine wisdom, which is innate to the aster and which provokes and inspires thought in the poet.

6. Why is the apostrophe used in line 14: 'But 'tis figured in the flowers'?

a) It is a typographical mistake.
b) To suggest the figure belongs to the flowers.
c) It is short for 'it is'.
d) It is short for 'it was'.

Answer: C

Again, this question is testing to see if we know the difference between a possessive apostrophe and one that is used in a contraction (when two words are squished together).

The correct answer here is (c): "'tis' is short for 'it is'.

This form of combing 'it' and 'is' is now uncommon – we tend to use 'it's' these days instead – yet you will still see it in slightly older pieces of writing.

7. What is it that the poet is suggesting the birds 'tell in their bowers'?

  a) **The fact that history is an illusion.**
  b) **The secret that all of history has taken place only in that forest.**
  c) **Wisdom akin to a kind of secret history.**
  d) **The song that the poet then sings at the end of the poem.**

Answer: C

What the poet tells us about these birds is in fact quite subtle and ambiguous. But remember: we are looking for the best answer – not necessarily a perfect answer – so we need to approach this question calmly.

Let's look at lines 15 and 16 in isolation:

  Was never secret history,
  But birds tell it in the bowers.

The poet at first seems to suggest that there is no such thing as a 'secret history' – which might mean something like a secret total wisdom of the universe – but then seems to say that, if there *was* such a thing as a 'secret history', then it would be what 'birds tell… in the bowers'.

He seems to be saying that, insofar as a secret history or wisdom might be said to exist, it can be found in the chatter of these birds.

Of the choices above, (c) is the best match, since it is saying that the birds in their bowers are saying something akin to a secret history.

Of all the other options, option **(a)** is a probably the sneakiest, because the phrase 'was never secret history' could arguably be interpreted as meaning that history is an illusion. However, this is something the poet is asserting; it is not something the birds are saying in their bower. As a result, **(a)** is incorrect.

8. Halfway through every sentence is a punctuation mark. What is this mark called?

  a) **Colon.**
  b) **Semi-colon.**
  c) **Comma.**
  d) **Ellipsis.**

Answer: B

In this poem, we can see that each stanza is a complete sentence, as each sentence finishes with a full stop. However, halfway through each stanza the poet uses a different piece of punctuation.

By way of an example, let's look at the final stanza:

  One harvest from thy field
  Homeward brought the oxen strong;
  A second crop thine acres yield,
  Which I gather in a song.

After the word strong, we have the punctuation mark in question. As already mentioned in the previous paper, it is a semi-colon: a piece of punctuation used to connect two ideas that are linked by their subject matter.

The upshot: **(b)** is the correct answer.

9. Why do you think the poet describes the 'acres' as yielding a 'second crop'?

  a) **The second crop refers to the wisdom the poet receives from the land.**
  b) **The acres are incredibly fertile so can produce two crops in one year.**

c) These are simply the lyrics to the song the poet is singing.
d) The second crop refers to the food the poet will eat himself.

Answer: A

Whereas the first crop was the physical, literal crop, the second one he is referring to is a metaphorical crop – namely, the knowledge or wisdom he gleans from the land – and thus (**a**) is correct.

Of the other options, (**c**) is the most likely to trip candidates. In a sense, the wisdom and knowledge the writer harvests from the land does seem to inspire the song he sings. However, the song is a by-product of the knowledge and wisdom metaphorically harvested from the land; and to claim that the poet is *only* harvesting the lyrics to the song is to neglect the most important thing the author is harvesting. (Also, we are not told that the song he sings has lyrics at all, which is a further clue that (**c**) is incorrect).

10. The first and third line in every stanza rhymes, and so too do the second and fourth line. How do you spell this technique?

    a) Alternate Ryme
    b) Alternate Ryme
    c) Allternate Rhyme
    d) Alternate Rhyme

Answer: D

Again, this is in fact a test of our spelling. The correct answer is (**d**). Remember: rhyme has that silent 'h' lurking within it!

The Extended Concentration Paper

The extended concentration paper in many ways resembles the scattershot paper. The key difference is that the extended concentration paper has nearly twice as many questions, and so it requires candidates to keep up their levels of focus over longer periods of time.

You will notice also that there are questions about more niche language techniques in these extended concentration papers. These are questions that are less likely to come up, but are modelled on questions that one does occasionally see in 11+ papers. In other words, if you can cope with the range of questions in the extended concentration paper, you will be well equipped to face any challenge the 11+ examiners might throw your way!

This extract is taken from the start of a short story set in early twentieth century America. It sees Nils Ericson head back to his hometown on the train.

1   The transcontinental express swung along the windings of the Sand River Valley, and
in the rear seat of the observation car a young man sat greatly at his ease, not in the
least discomfited by the fierce sunlight which beat in upon his brown face and neck
and strong back. There was a look of relaxation and of great passivity about his
5   broad shoulders, which seemed almost too heavy until he stood up and squared them.
He wore a pale flannel shirt and a blue silk necktie with loose ends. His trousers were
wide and belted at the waist, and his short sack coat hung open. His heavy shoes had
seen good service. His reddish-brown hair, like his clothes, had a foreign cut. He had
deep-set, dark blue eyes under heavy reddish eyebrows. His face was kept clean only
10   by close shaving, and even the sharpest razor left a glint of yellow in the smooth
brown of his skin. His teeth and the palms of his hands were very white. His head,
which looked hard and stubborn, lay indolently in the green cushion of the wicker
chair, and as he looked out at the ripe summer country a teasing, not unkindly smile
played over his lips. Once, as he basked thus comfortably, a quick light flashed in his
15   eyes, curiously dilating the pupils, and his mouth became a hard, straight line, gradu-
ally relaxing into its former smile of rather kindly mockery. He told himself, apparently, that there was no point in getting excited; and he seemed a master hand at
taking his ease when he could. Neither the sharp whistle of the locomotive nor the
brakeman's call disturbed him. It was not until after the train had stopped that he

20 rose, put on a Panama hat, took from the rack a small valise and a flute case, and stepped deliberately to the station platform. The baggage was already unloaded, and the stranger presented a check for a battered sole-leather steamer trunk.

"Can you keep it here for a day or two?" he asked the agent. "I may send for it, and I may not."

25 "Depends on whether you like the country, I suppose?" demanded the agent in a challenging tone.

"Just so."

The agent shrugged his shoulders, looked scornfully at the small trunk, which was marked "N.E.," and handed out a claim check without further comment. The
30 stranger watched him as he caught one end of the trunk and dragged it into the express room. The agent's manner seemed to remind him of something amusing. "Doesn't seem to be a very big place," he remarked, looking about.

"It's big enough for us," snapped the agent, as he banged the trunk into a corner.

That remark, apparently, was what Nils Ericson had wanted. He chuckled quietly as
35 he took a leather strap from his pocket and swung his valise around his shoulder. Then he settled his Panama securely on his head, turned up his trousers, tucked the flute case under his arm, and started off across the fields. He gave the town, as he would have said, a wide berth, and cut through a great fenced pasture, emerging, when he rolled under the barbed wire at the farther corner, upon a white dusty road
40 which ran straight up from the river valley to the high prairies, where the ripe wheat stood yellow and the tin roofs and weathercocks were twinkling in the fierce sunlight. By the time Nils had done three miles, the sun was sinking and the farm wagons on their way home from town came rattling by, covering him with dust and making him sneeze. When one of the farmers pulled up and offered to give him a lift, he clam-
45 bered in willingly.

The driver was a thin, grizzled old man with a long lean neck and a foolish sort of beard, like a goat's. "How fur ye goin'?" he asked, as he clucked to his horses and started off.

"Do you go by the Ericson place?"

50 "Which Ericson?" The old man drew in his reins as if he expected to stop again.

"Preacher Ericson's."

"Oh, the Old Lady Ericson's!" He turned and looked at Nils. "La, me! If you're goin' out there you might a' rid out in the automobile. That's a pity, now. The Old Lady Ericson was in town with her auto. You might 'a' heard it snortin' anywhere about the
55 post-office er the butcher shop."

"Has she a motor?" asked the stranger absently.

"'Deed an' she has! She runs into town every night about this time for her mail and meat for supper. Some folks say she's afraid her auto won't get exercise enough, but I say that's jealousy."

60   "Aren't there any other motors about here?"

"Oh, yes! we have fourteen in all. But nobody else gets around like the Old Lady Ericson. She's out, rain er shine, over the whole county, chargin' into town and out amongst her farms, an' up to her sons' places. Sure you ain't goin' to the wrong place?" He craned his neck and looked at Nils' flute case with eager curiosity. "The
65   old woman ain't got any piany that I knows on. Olaf, he has a grand. His wife's musical: took lessons in Chicago."

"I'm going up there tomorrow," said Nils imperturbably. He saw that the driver took him for a piano tuner.

"Oh, I see!" The old man screwed up his eyes mysteriously. He was a little dashed by
70   the stranger's noncommunicativeness, but he soon broke out again.

"I'm one o' Mrs Ericson's tenants. Look after one of her places. I did own the place myself once, but I lost it a while back, in the bad years just after the World's Fair. Just as well, too, I say. Lets you out o' payin' taxes. The Ericsons do own most of the county now. Listen, if that ain't the old woman comin' now. Want I should stop her?"

75 Nils shook his head. He heard the deep chug-chug of a motor vibrating steadily in the clear twilight behind them. The pale lights of the car swam over the hill, and the old man slapped his reins and turned clear out of the road, ducking his head at the first of three angry snorts from behind. The motor was running at a hot, even speed, and passed without turning an inch from its course. The driver was a stalwart woman
80   who sat at ease in the front seat and drove her car bareheaded. She left a cloud of dust and a trail of gasoline behind her. Her tenant threw back his head and sneezed.

An extract adapted from Willa Cather's 'The Bohemian Girl'

---

1. What terrain is the transcontinental express passing through at the start of this extract?

    a) A flat plain.
    b) A mountain pass.
    c) A valley.
    d) A marshland.

Answer: ___

2. '[he was] not in the least discomfited by the fierce sunlight'

What does this mean?

    a) The strength of the sunlight was very uncomfortable for Nils.
    b) Nils took huge amount of pleasure from the sunlight beating on him.
    c) Although the sunlight was strong, it did not make Nils feel uncomfortable.
    d) Nils was not the least uncomfortable of everyone experiencing the sunlight.

Answer: ___

3. 'There was a look of relaxation and of great passivity about his shoulders'

What is another way of saying 'passivity'?

    a) Gravitas.
    b) Tension.
    c) Inactivity.
    d) Excitement.

Answer: ___

4. What colour hair does Nils Ericson have?

    a) Reddish-brown.
    b) Red.
    c) Black.
    d) Blonde.

Answer: ___

5. The author describes the light as 'dilating' Nils's pupils (line 15). What does this word suggest about Nils's pupils?

    a) His pupils make him look as if he has died.
    b) His pupils have expanded.
    c) His pupils have contracted.
    d) His pupils have taken on a look of greater intensity.

Answer: ___

6. 'he seemed a master hand at taking his ease when he could.'

What does this phrase suggest about Nils?

    a) Nils was very skilled at making people he met feel relaxed.
    b) When relaxing, Nils would lean on his dominant hand.
    c) Nils was known for stealing items from others when he could.
    d) Nils was skilled at relaxing when an opportunity presented itself.

                                               Answer: ___

7. What is meant by 'locomotive'?

    a) A train conductor.
    b) A train's inbuilt air whistle.
    c) A train.
    d) A person's inner conscience.

                                               Answer: ___

8. How does Nils react to the brakeman's call?

    a) He rises and puts on his Panama hat.
    b) A not unkindly smile plays over his lips.
    c) He gives himself a close shave with a razor.
    d) Nils does not react to the brakeman's call.

                                               Answer: ___

9. How many adjectives can you count in the sentence beginning "He chuckled quietly…"?

    a) 1
    b) 2
    c) 3
    d) 5

                                               Answer: ___

10. 'looked scornfully at the small trunk'

Which of the following words is closest in meaning to 'scornfully'?

a) Contemptuously.
b) Jealously.
c) Indifferently.
d) Tiredly.

Answer: ___

11. Why does Nils leave his trunk with the agent?

a) Nils trusts the agent to look after it more than anyone else in town.
b) It contains his flute, which is too heavy to carry.
c) Nils has a shoulder injury.
d) He is not yet sure whether he wishes to stay in this town for a prolonged period.

Answer: ___

12. Where does the agent place Nils's trunk?

a) The corner office.
b) The express room.
c) The station platform.
d) On a wicker chair.

Answer: ___

13. 'He gave the town, as he would have said, a wide berth'

What does this suggest about Nils's attitude towards the town?

a) He feels fondly towards it because it was where he was born.
b) A wide berth means a dirty look, so Nils dislikes the town.
c) He wishes to keep distance between himself and the town.
d) He considers it a place where he would like to spend his time.

Answer: ___

14. How does Nils get out of the 'great fenced pasture'? (line 38)

a) He climbs over the barbed wire fence.
b) He rolls under the barbed wire.
c) He swings his valise at the fencing.
d) He cut through the barbed wire fencing.

Answer: ____

15. Why did Nils opt to get in the carriage with the farmer?

a) Nils was physically exhausted after having walked for three miles.
b) Nils wanted to be shielded from the pollen that was making him sneeze.
c) Nils wanted to talk to the farmer about Lady Ericson.
d) The sun was setting and the dust on the road was making him sneeze.

Answer: ____

16. What does the word 'grizzled' suggest about the driver in line 46?

a) That he looks like a grizzly bear.
b) That he has greying hair.
c) That he looks exhausted.
d) That he has a contrary expression on his face.

Answer: ____

17. The farmer had 'a foolish sort of beard, like a goat's' (lines 46-47)

This is an example of:

a) A metaphor.
b) Personification.
c) Alliteration.
d) A simile.

Answer: ____

18. Based on the passage, what is Nils's intended destination for this journey?

a) Olaf's house.
b) Chicago.
c) The post office.
d) Lady Ericson's house.

Answer: ____

19. What is the object of the phrase: 'he clucked to his horses'.

a) He
b) Clucked
c) His
d) Horses

Answer: ___

20. 'asked the stranger absently'

What does the word 'absently' say about Nils's tone here?

a) His tone is highly engaged.
b) His tone is conveying a degree of excitement.
c) His tone makes him sound lonely.
d) His tone is highly disengaged.

Answer: ___

21. What type of words are the following? 'quietly' (line 34), securely (line 36), willingly (line 45), mysteriously (line 69), 'steadily' (line 75)

a) Adjectives.
b) Adverbs.
c) Nouns.
d) Prepositions.

Answer: ___

22. Why does the farmer think Nils might be a piano tuner?

a) Because Nils has a flute, which makes him seem adept with instruments.
b) Because Nils is heading to Olaf's house, where there is a grand piano.
c) Because Nils tells him he works with musical instruments for a living.
d) Because Nils looks physically very similar to the town's piano tuner.

Answer: ___

23. 'He craned his neck and looked at Nils' flute case with eager curiosity'.

Which word is the pronoun in this sentence?

a) He
b) Nils
c) Flute
d) Neck

Answer: ___

24. Which word is the proper noun in the following sentence: 'His wife's musical: took lessons in Chicago.'

a) Wife
b) Musical
c) Lessons
d) Chicago

Answer: ___

25. What do we know about the weather on the day in which this passage is set?

a) The pollen count was exceptionally high, causing people to sneeze.
b) The sun had been fierce almost right up until sunset.
c) It had been a cold day that had required Nils to wear a panama hat.
d) It had been raining, which is why Mrs Ericson had chosen to drive.

Answer: ___

26. What type of words are the following? 'relaxing' (line 16) 'disturbed' (line 19) 'tucked' (line 36) 'clucked' (line 47) 'started' (line 48) .

a) Adverbs.
b) Adjectives.
c) Prepositions.
d) Verbs.

Answer: ___

27. According to the farmer, how do some of the townspeople respond to the frequency of Mrs Ericson's driving expeditions?

a) They cheer her on since the car helps the local economy.
b) They snort whenever they see her driving to show their disapproval.

c) They mock her as someone who treats her car as if it were a living thing.
d) They charge at her car whenever they see it to show their disapproval.

Answer: ___

28. How many cars are there in this area?

a) One.
b) Two.
c) Fourteen.
d) Fifteen.

Answer: ___

29. Why, according to the farmer, is it a good thing that he lost his place? (lines 71-73)

a) It allowed him to pursue a career in farming.
b) It reduced his tax burden.
c) The upkeep had been too stressful.
d) It allowed him to spend more time with his family.

Answer: ___

30. What would be another word for 'imperturbably' on line 67?

a) Composedly.
b) Angrily.
c) Genially.
d) Agitatedly.

Answer: ___

31. What type of word is 'noncommunicativeness' on line 70?

a) Adjunct.
b) Noun.
c) Adjective.
d) Verb.

Answer: ___

32. "'I'm one o' Mrs Ericson's tenants.'"

What is the subject of the sentence?

    a) One
    b) I
    c) Tenants
    d) Mrs Ericson

                                    Answer: ___

33. What of the following words is used interchangeably with 'car' in this passage?

    a) Engine.
    b) Motor.
    c) Carriage.
    d) Horse.

                                    Answer: ___

34. Which word does *not* describe the farmer?

    a) Talkative.
    b) Curious.
    c) Unguarded.
    d) Surly.

                                    Answer: ___

35. Which of these statements is true?

    a) Mrs Ericson is the farmer's tenant.
    b) Nils is Mrs Ericson's tenant.
    c) The farmer used to Mrs Ericson's tenant, but is no longer.
    d) The farmer is Mrs Ericson's tenant.

                                    Answer: ___

36. 'He heard the deep chug-chug of a motor'

What technique is used in this phrase?

a) Metaphor.
b) Anthropomorphisation.
c) Scansion.
d) Onomatopoeia.

Answer: ___

37. What does the driver do once Mrs Ericson overtakes him in her car?

a) He tells Nils about the World's Fair.
b) He pulls over to the side of the road.
c) He slaps his reins.
d) He sneezes.

Answer: ___

38. What tense is the extract written in?

a) Past tense.
b) Present tense.
c) Future tense.
d) None of the above.

Answer: ___

39. Who is the narrator of this extract?

a) Nils.
b) The driver.
c) Mrs Ericson.
d) None of the above.

Answer: ___

40. Which of these statements matches the end of the extract?

a) Mrs Ericson is fleeing from Nils.
b) Nils is now unable to go to Mrs Ericson's home.
c) The driver has managed to get Mrs Ericson to pull over.
d) Nils has spotted the woman whose home he is heading to.

Answer: ___

1. What terrain is the transcontinental express passing through at the start of this extract?

    a) A flat plain.
    b) A mountain pass.
    c) A valley.
    d) A marshland.

                                                          Answer: C

We are back in the realm of fairly straightforward retrieval here.

In the opening sentence we are told that the train is going 'along the windings of the Sand River Valley'. From this we know that **(c)** is correct: the train is passing through a valley.

2. '[he was] not in the least discomfited by the fierce sunlight'

What does this mean?

    a) The strength of the sunlight was very uncomfortable for Nils.

b) Nils took huge amount of pleasure from the sunlight beating on him.

c) Although the sunlight was strong, it did not make Nils feel uncomfortable.

d) Nils was not the least uncomfortable of everyone experiencing the sunlight.

Answer: C

Another style of question we often see in 11+ resembles the question above: an entire quote is laid out, and then a question about the quote follows. Yet while the format has changed, it is not really doing anything too different to other questions we have seen in previous papers.

We are, in effect, being ask to demonstrate our understanding of a particular section of text, and we have been in this territory before.

To be discomfited means to be made uncomfortable. However, we are being told that Nils was 'not in the least discomfited' by the 'fierce' sunlight, which means he was *not* being made uncomfortable by the powerful sunlight. Option (**c**), then, is correct.

Option (**d**) is the one most likely to trip students up, as it uses the phrase 'not the least uncomfortable'. However, if we read option (**d**) carefully, we can see that it is *not* simply saying that Nils wasn't made uncomfortable by the powerful sun – instead, it is comparing Nils's experience of the sunlight to other people's experience – and it is therefore incorrect.

3. 'There was a look of relaxation and of great passivity about his shoulders'

What is another way of saying 'passivity'?

a) Gravitas.
b) Tension.
c) Inactivity.
d) Excitement.

Answer: C

To be passive is to allow things to happen to you: it sort of means the opposite of active. Thus option **(c)** is our best option here: Nils's shoulders have an air of simply allowing things to happen to them and therefore being, in a sense, inactive.

4. What colour hair does Nils Ericson have?

    a) **Reddish-brown.**
    b) **Red.**
    c) **Black.**
    d) **Blonde.**

Answer: A

At line 8, we are told of Nils's 'reddish-brown hair'. Option **(a)**, then, is correct.

5. The author describes the light as 'dilating' Nils's pupils (line 15). What does this word suggest about Nils's pupils?

    a) **His pupils make him look as if he has died.**
    b) **His pupils have expanded.**
    c) **His pupils have contracted.**
    d) **His pupils have taken on a look of greater intensity.**

Answer: B

This is a definition-style question: it is testing your understanding of the word 'dilating'. If a pupil dilates, it means it expands, and thus **(b)** is the correct answer.

The tricky thing about this question is the context, which could potentially confuse candidates. Your pupil dilates when there is less light, for this allows more light in. Yet in the extract we are told that 'a quick light flashed in his eyes, curiously dilating the pupils', which could seem contradictory: after all, pupils dilate when there is less light, not more. However, the writer is in fact describing the moments *after* the light flashed in Nils's eyes, and the way Nils's pupils readjusted to the *absence* of that flash of light.

6. 'he seemed a master hand at taking his ease when he could.'

What does this phrase suggest about Nils?

   a) Nils was very skilled at making people he met feel relaxed.
   b) When relaxing, Nils would lean on his dominant hand.
   c) Nils was known for stealing items from others when he could.
   d) Nils was skilled at relaxing when an opportunity presented itself.

Answer: D

To be a 'master hand' at something means to be an expert or very skilled at it. More-over, to be at ease means to be relaxed, and thus to take one's ease refers to an individual's ability to allow themselves to relax.

We are being told, in short, that Nils is skilled at being able to relax when given a chance, which corresponds with option (**d**).

7. What is meant by 'locomotive'?

   a) A train conductor.
   b) A train's inbuilt air whistle.
   c) A train.
   d) A person's inner conscience.

Answer: C

A 'locomotive' is another word for a train, so (**c**) is the correct answer.

8. How does Nils react to the brakeman's call?

   a) He rises and puts on his Panama hat.
   b) A not unkindly smile plays over his lips.
   c) He gives himself a close shave with a razor.
   d) Nils does not react to the brakeman's call.

Answer: D

At lines 18-19, we learn that 'neither the sharp whistle of the locomotive nor the brakeman's call disturbed him'. If it did not disturb him, the implication is that he did not react to it, and thus **(d)** is correct.

Notice how options **(a)** and **(b)** describe other actions that Nils performs, but, crucially, they are *not* in response to the brakeman's call. The examiner has put these in intentionally to catch out those students who recognize these details as having appeared in the text, but who have not taken care to check *when* they appear.

9. How many adjectives can you count in the sentence beginning "He chuckled quietly..."?

    a) 1
    b) 2
    c) 3
    d) 5

Answer: A

The only adjective in this sentence is the word 'leather', and thus **(a)** is the correct answer. Some students might have picked out 'quietly', but it is in fact an adverb, since it is describing a verb, not a noun.

10. 'looked scornfully at the small trunk'

Which of the following words is closest in meaning to 'scornfully'?

    a) Contemptuously.
    b) Jealously.
    c) Indifferently.
    d) Tiredly.

Answer: A

This is a definition-style question; however, whereas in other papers we need to go and check the context ourselves, the examiner is doing some of the leg work for us by including the quote in the question.

To be scornful of something is to be contemptuous of it. It means something akin to 'looking down on' something. Option (**a**), then, is the correct answer.

11. Why does Nils leave his trunk with the agent?

> a) **Nils trusts the agent to look after it more than anyone else in town.**
> b) **It contains his flute, which is too heavy to carry.**
> c) **Nils has a shoulder injury.**
> d) **He is not yet sure whether he wishes to stay in this town for a prolonged period.**

Answer: D

After Nils tells the agent that he might send for his trunk, but also that he might not, the agent asks whether it's because Nils was waiting to see if he liked the area enough to hang around: 'Depends on whether you like the country, I suppose?' In response to this query, Nils confirms that this is the case: 'Just so'.

This is the best evidence we have as to why Nils leaves his trunk with the agent; and the option that best matches this is (**d**), which states that Nils is not sure yet whether he wishes to stay in this town for a prolonged period of time.

12. Where does the agent place Nils's trunk?

> a) **The corner office.**
> b) **The express room.**
> c) **The station platform.**
> d) **On a wicker chair.**

Answer: B

We are told at lines 30-31 that the agent 'caught one end of the trunk and dragged it into the express room', and, at line 33, that he 'banged the trunk into a corner'. Ergo: the trunk ends up in the corner or the express room, and thus **(b)** is correct.

Option **(a)** is trying to catch us out: after all, the word 'corner' does appear during this section regarding Nils's trunk, but at no point are we told that the bag is placed in a corner office.

13. 'He gave the town, as he would have said, a wide berth'

What does this suggest about Nils's attitude towards the town?

  a) He feels fondly towards it because it was where he was born.
  b) A wide berth means a dirty look, so Nils dislikes the town.
  c) He wishes to keep distance between himself and the town.
  d) He considers it a place where he would like to spend his time.

Answer: C

Giving something a wide berth means keeping a distance from it, or trying to avoid it altogether. As such, option **(c)** is correct.

14. How does Nils get out of the 'great fenced pasture'? (line 38)

  a) He climbs over the barbed wire fence.
  b) He rolls under the barbed wire.
  c) He swings his valise at the fencing.
  d) He cut through the barbed wire fencing.

Answer: B

Let's take a look at the section of text where Nils goes through the fenced pasture, and then exits it:

'[Nils] cut through a great fenced pasture, emerging, when he rolled under the barbed wire at the farther corner, upon a white dusty road'.

As we can see, Nils leaves the 'great fenced pasture' and emerges on the 'white dusty road' after having 'rolled under the barbed wire', which matches up with option **(b)** – the correct answer.

Notice how option **(d)** uses the phrase 'cut through' to try and trip us up. However, Nils cuts through the pasture, not the fence itself – hence **(d)** is incorrect.

15. Why did Nils opt to get in the carriage with the farmer?

    a) **Nils was physically exhausted after having walked for three miles.**
    b) **Nils wanted to be shielded from the pollen that was making him sneeze.**
    c) **Nils wanted to talk to the farmer about Lady Ericson.**
    d) **The sun was setting and the dust on the road was making him sneeze.**

Answer: D

At lines 42-44, just before Nils accepts a ride from the farmer, we have the following sentence:

'By the time Nils had done three miles, the sun was sinking and the farm wagons on their way home from town came rattling by, covering him with dust and making him sneeze.'

It seems, judging from this sentence, that it was the setting of the sun and the dust on the road that most concerned Nils, and thus its logical to deduce that it were these two things that motivated him to accept the ride. This tallies with option **(d)**.

16. What does the word 'grizzled' suggest about the driver in line 46?

    a) **That he looks like a grizzly bear.**
    b) **That he has greying hair.**
    c) **That he looks exhausted.**
    d) **That he has a contrary expression on his face.**

Answer: B

To be grizzled is to have grey or greying hair. Therefore, option **(b)** is the correct answer.

17. The farmer had 'a foolish sort of beard, like a goat's' (line 46-47)

This is an example of:

a) A metaphor.
b) Personification.
c) Alliteration.
d) A simile

Answer: D

We have a comparison here which makes itself explicit using the word 'like'; as a result, we know this is a simile, and thus **(d)** is the correct answer.

Note that if we had been told instead that the farmer 'had a foolish goat's beard', this would have been a metaphor instead, as the comparison between the farmer's beard and that of a goat's would have been implicit. However, since this isn't the case, we know the examiner is not looking for **(a)**.

Remember that personification is when non-human entities are given human attributes. Yet this is not the case here. On the contrary: we have a human being given an animalistic attribute instead! Option **(b)**, then, is also incorrect.

Alliteration is when you have words beginning with the same letter (for instance: the blue boy begged balefully). However, as this technique is not used in the quote above, option **(c)** is incorrect.

18. Based on the passage, what is Nils's intended destination for this journey?

a) Olaf's house.
b) Chicago.
c) The post office.
d) Lady Ericson's house.

Answer: D

At line 49, when Nils first encounters the farmer, Nils asks: 'Do you go by the Ericson place?' From this we can infer that his destination is the Ericson's house. The farmer – at line 52 – then clarifies for the reader that Nils is referring to the home of Lady Ericson ('the Old Lady Ericson'). Given that this dialogue is taking place at the point at which the farmer is agreeing to give Nils a ride, it is self-evident that Lady Ericson's house is Nils's destination for this journey. Option (**d**), then, is correct.

You might notice that a little later on, after the farmer discusses both Olaf's house and Chicago, Nils responds that he is 'going up there tomorrow'. It is almost certain that he is referring to Olaf's house as opposed to Chicago; but either way, neither Olaf's house nor Chicago are the destination of *this* journey, and thus (**a**) and (**b**) are both incorrect.

19. What is the object of the phrase: 'he clucked to his horses'.

   a) He
   b) Clucked
   c) His
   d) Horses

Answer: D

The object of a sentence or phrase is the person or thing on the receiving end of the verb. The horses are on the receiving end of the verb ('clucked'), and thus (**d**) is correct – the word 'horses' is the object of the sentence.

20. 'asked the stranger absently'

What does the word 'absently' say about Nils's tone here?

   a) His tone is highly engaged.
   b) His tone is conveying a degree of excitement.
   c) His tone makes him sound lonely.
   d) His tone is highly disengaged.

Answer: D

Absent means the opposite of present. To be literally absent means to not be somewhere at all – so, if a classmate was not at school because they were sick, you might say they were absent.

However, to be metaphorically absent is to be disengaged or detached from what is going on around you. Therefore, to speak absently is to speak in a way that suggests you are disengaged or detached from the conversation. As such, (**d**) is the correct answer.

21. What type of words are the following? 'quietly' (line 34), securely (line 36), willingly (line 45), mysteriously (line 69), 'steadily' (line 75)

   a) **Adjectives.**
   b) **Adverbs.**
   c) **Nouns.**
   d) **Prepositions.**

Answer: B

The correct answer here is (**b**), these are adverbs.

Remember that an adverb is a type of describing word that is used to describe *not* a noun, but a verb or adjective or phrase, and they often (though not always) end with the letters 'ly'. On this occasion, however, all of these adverbs do indeed end with 'ly'!

As an aside, a preposition is a word that tells us where or when something is in relation to another thing. Examples include words such as 'inside', 'outside', 'under', 'on', 'before', 'after'.

22. Why does the farmer think Nils might be a piano tuner?

   a) **Because Nils has a flute, which makes him seem adept with instruments.**
   b) **Because Nils is heading to Olaf's house, where there is a grand piano.**

c) **Because Nils tells him he works with musical instruments for a living.**

d) **Because Nils looks physically very similar to the town's piano tuner.**

Answer: A

At line 64, we hear that the farmer 'craned his neck and looked at Nils' flute case with eager curiosity', and, after this, he starts talking about Olaf's grand piano. From this we can infer that the driver takes Nils for a piano tuner on account of the fact he is carrying a musical instrument (a flute) and thus seems as though he is at home with musical instruments in general. Ergo: option (**a**) is correct.

We can also confirm that (**a**) is correct by eliminating the other options.

Option (**b**) suggests that the farmer thinks Nils might be a piano tuner because he is going to Olaf's house. However, the farmer only learns that Nils is intending to visit Olaf's at line 67 – after the farmer already seems to have decided Nils might be a piano tuner – hence this could not be what made the farmer think this way.

Option (**c**) is incorrect, because at no point does Nils claim to work with musical instruments for a living. Moreover, there is no evidence whatsoever in the passage that Nils looks similar to the town's piano tuner, let alone that the town even has a resident piano tuner, meaning (**d**) is also incorrect.

---

23. 'He craned his neck and looked at Nils' flute case with eager curiosity'.

Which word is the pronoun in this sentence?

a) **He**
b) **Nils**
c) **Flute**
d) **Neck**

Answer: A

As mentioned earlier, a pronoun is a word that substitutes in for a noun in certain contexts, and examples include 'he', 'she', 'they', 'him', 'she', 'them', and so on. Option (**a**), then, is the correct answer here.

24. Which word is the proper noun in the following sentence: 'His wife's musical: took lessons in Chicago.'

  a) **Wife**
  b) **Musical**
  c) **Lessons**
  d) **Chicago**

Answer: D

A proper noun is a name given to a specific place, person or thing. As such, option (**d**), Chicago, is the correct answer.

Other proper nouns in the text would include 'Nils', 'Olaf' and 'Ericson'.

25. What do we know about the weather on the day in which this passage is set?

  a) **The pollen count was exceptionally high, causing people to sneeze.**
  b) **The sun had been fierce almost right up until sunset.**
  c) **It had been a cold day that had required Nils to wear a panama hat.**
  d) **It had been raining, which is why Mrs Ericson had chosen to drive.**

Answer: B

The reader learns of the fierce sun in the opening paragraph ('fierce sunlight' is mentioned at line 3) and we see the phrase 'fierce sunlight' appear for a second time at line 41, during Nils's walk from the station. In the following sentence, the sun then sets. The upshot: the weather in the passage is characterised by fierce sunshine right up until sunset – as option (**b**) asserts.

. . .

26. What type of words are the following? 'relaxing' (line 16) 'disturbed' (line 19) 'tucked' (line 36) 'clucked' (line 47) 'started' (line 48).

    a) Adverbs.
    b) Adjectives.
    c) Prepositions.
    d) Verbs.

Answer: D

These words are all types of verbs, which we might think of as 'doing' words; as such, (**d**) is correct.

27. According to the farmer, how do some of the townspeople respond to the frequency of Mrs Ericson's driving expeditions?

    a) They cheer her on since the car helps the local economy.
    b) They snort whenever they see her driving to show their disapproval.
    c) They mock her as someone who treats her car as if it were a living thing.
    d) They charge at her car whenever they see it to show their disapproval.

Answer: C

At lines 58-59, as the farmer discusses Mrs Ericson's driving habits, he says the following:

'Some folks say she's afraid her auto won't get exercise enough, but I say that's jealousy.'

Cars are, of course, *not* living things, but 'some folks', according to the farmer, teasingly suggest that the reason Mrs Ericson drives her car so much is because she is 'afraid' it 'won't get exercise enough' – as if she cares for it in the same over-the-top way you might, say, a pet dog. That these comments are intended to mock Mrs

Ericson is revealed by the farmer's final thought that they are the product of 'jealousy'.

With all this in mind, **(c)** clearly stands out as the correct answer.

28. How many cars are there in this area?

    a) One.
    b) Two.
    c) Fourteen.
    d) Fifteen.

Answer: C

At line 61, in response to Nils's enquiry regarding the cars in the area, the farmer says the following: 'we have fourteen in all'. In light of this, **(c)** is the correct answer.

29. Why, according to the farmer, is it a good thing that he lost his place? (line 71-73)

    a) It allowed him to pursue a career in farming.
    b) It reduced his tax burden.
    c) The upkeep had been too stressful.
    d) It allowed him to spend more time with his family.

Answer: B

At line 72, the farmer says that he 'lost' his place 'just after the World's Fair', then immediately goes on to claim that it is 'just as well, too' because it 'lets you out o' payin' taxes'. In other words, he is saying that it is, in a sense, a good thing that he lost ownership of his home, since it means he does not have to pay taxes on the property, thereby reducing his tax burden. Ergo: **(b)** is the correct answer.

30. What would be another word for 'imperturbably' on line 67?

    a) Composedly.

b) Angrily.
c) Genially.
d) Agitatedly.

Answer: A

If someone is perturbed, it means they are unsettled or have lost their composure. To be unperturbed means the opposite: it means to be composed and unfazed. So, when Nils is said to say something 'imperturbably' at line 67, it means that he speaks with composure, or 'composedly', as option (**a**) puts it.

31. What type of word is 'noncommunicativeness' on line 70?

    a) Adjunct.
    b) Noun.
    c) Adjective.
    d) Verb.

Answer: B

If Nils had been described as 'noncommunicative', this would be an adjective, since the word would be used to directly describe him. However, 'noncommunicativeness' is a noun, since it refers to one of Nils's qualities /attributes, and thus (**b**) is correct.

As an aside, the word 'adjunct' is used to describe a secondary or less important detail in a sentence. If I were to say 'they placed a delicious pie on the counter', the phrase 'the counter' could be called the adjunct.

32. "'I'm one o' Mrs Ericson's tenants.'"

What is the subject of the sentence?

    a) One
    b) I
    c) Tenants
    d) Mrs Ericson

Answer: B

The subject of a sentence is the person or thing in the sentence either doing or being. Here, the subject is 'I': the farmer is the subject, and he is talking about his state of being Mrs Ericson's tenant. Accordingly, **(b)** is the correct answer.

As mentioned already, the object of the sentence, on the other hand, is the person or thing that is on the receiving end of the action of the verb. In this instance, 'Mrs Ericson' is the object of the sentence.

33. What of the following words is used interchangeably with 'car' in this passage?

    a) **Engine.**
    b) **Motor.**
    c) **Carriage.**
    d) **Horse.**

Answer: B

The word motor is used multiple times to refer to the car: 'Has she a motor'; 'any other motors'; 'chug-chug of a motor'; 'the motor was running at a hot, even speed'. Option **(b)**, then, is the correct answer.

As an aside (though you don't need to know this to score the mark here), the literary technique of using a part of something (for instance, a motor) to describe the entire thing (for instance, a car) is known as synecdoche.

34. Which word does *not* describe the farmer?

    a) **Talkative.**
    b) **Curious.**
    c) **Unguarded.**
    d) **Surly.**

Answer: D

With a question like this – where we are being asked to identify the option that does not apply – the process of elimination is our best path forward.

The farmer definitely seems to be talkative. At one point, for instance, after trying and failing to engage Nils in conversation, he attempts to persevere with his chatting all the same: 'He was a little dashed by the stranger's noncommunicativeness, but he soon broke out again'. As a result, we can eliminate (**a**).

At line 64, we learn that the farmer 'craned his neck and looked at Nils' flute case with eager curiosity'. The phrase 'eager curiosity' makes it difficult to argue with the notion that the farmer is curious, and thus we can also eliminate (**b**).

To be unguarded means to not suspect others and to share openly with others in a candid way. The very fact that the farmer gives Nils – a complete stranger – a ride suggests he is unguarded. Moreover, that the farmer happily shares a good deal of intimate information with Nils – the fact he lost his property, for instance; his living circumstances, too – again suggests he is unguarded. Option (**c**), then, can be eliminated.

To be surly means to be irritable and grumpy. However, the driver seems very patient and hospitable to Nils, and not at all surly. Option (**d**) therefore stands out as the correct answer.

35. Which of these statements is true?

a) Mrs Ericson is the farmer's tenant.
b) Nils is Mrs Ericson's tenant.
c) The farmer used to Mrs Ericson's tenant, but is no longer.
d) The farmer is Mrs Ericson's tenant.

Answer: D

At line 71, the farmer say 'I'm one o' Mrs Ericson's tenants'. This tells us that, of the options above, (**d**) is the correct answer.

36. 'He heard the deep chug-chug of a motor'

What technique is used in this phrase?

a) **Metaphor.**
b) **Anthropomorphisation.**
c) **Scansion.**
d) **Onomatopoeia.**

Answer: D

As mentioned previously, onomatopoeia is when you have a word that audibly sounds like the thing it is describing. The motor in an engine makes a 'chug-chug' sound, and thus this is an example of onomatopoeia and (**d**) is the correct answer.

Now, let's eliminate the other options for the sake of extra clarity.

A metaphor is an implicit comparison. There is no such comparison here, however, so (**a**) is also incorrect.

Anthropomorphisation is very similar to personification. It is when non-human entities are given human characteristics. Again, this is not present in this quote, so (**b**) is incorrect.

Scansion is not in fact a literary technique: it is when you read some poetry and try and work out the rhythm. So (**c**), too, is incorrect.

37. What does the driver do once Mrs Ericson overtakes him in her car?

a) **He tells Nils about the World's Fair.**
b) **He pulls over to the side of the road.**
c) **He slaps his reins.**
d) **He sneezes.**

Answer: D

Mrs Ericson overtakes the farmer in the final paragraph, and what the farmer does immediately afterwards is spelt out in the passage's final sentence: 'Her tenant threw back his head and sneezed.' Ergo, (**d**) is the correct answer.

The other options are all things the farmer does, but, crucially, *before* he is overtaken by Mrs Ericson, and thus are all incorrect.

· · ·

38. What tense is the extract written in?

    a) Past tense.
    b) Present tense.
    c) Future tense.
    d) None of the above.

Answer: A

The correct answer is (**a**), the past tense. It is instructive to take a sentence from the extract to help illustrate this:

'The old man screwed up his eyes mysteriously'.

This is written in the past tense. However, if it had been written in the present tense, it would look like this:

'The old man screws up his eyes mysteriously'.

Finally, if it had been written in the future tense, it would look like this:

'The old man will screw up his eyes mysteriously'.

When faced with a question about tense, my advice is always to look at the verbs. Are these actions that have already taken place? Are they taking place now? Or are they going to take place in the future?

39. Who is the narrator of this extract?

    a) Nils.
    b) The driver.
    c) Mrs Ericson.
    d) None of the above.

Answer: D

The correct answer is (**d**), since it is written in the third person, and not by any one character.

A third person narrative is when the narrator seems to be watching the characters and describing their actions and thoughts, but is not part of the story. Phrases like 'he did this' and 'she did that' are what you might see in a third person narrative.

If one of the characters were telling the story, it would be written in the first person ('I did this'; 'I did that'). However, because none of the characters are telling the story and this piece is *not* written in the first person, options **(a)**, **(b)** and **(c)** are all incorrect.

40. Which of these statements matches the end of the extract?

    a) Mrs Ericson is fleeing from Nils.
    b) Nils is now unable to go to Mrs Ericson's home.
    c) The driver has managed to get Mrs Ericson to pull over.
    d) Nils has spotted the woman whose home he is heading to.

Answer: D

A question of this kind – where we are being asked to decide which option best matches a portion of the extract (in this case, the end) – lends itself to the process of elimination.

Option **(a)** suggests that Mrs Ericson is fleeing from Nils. However, there is no evidence that Mrs Ericson is even aware of Nils's presence, and there is no evidence whatsoever that she is fleeing him when she overtakes the horse-drawn carriage in the final paragraph. From this we can extrapolate that **(a)** is incorrect.

There is also no evidence that, just because Mrs Ericson has overtaken Nils and the farmer, that he is now unable to go to her home. As such, option **(b)** is also incorrect.

Whereas **(c)** suggests the farmer has managed to get Mrs Ericson to pull over, in fact the opposite is true: Mrs Ericson, by coming up behind the farmer, causes the farmer to pull over. And although the farmer enquires whether Nils would like him to try and pull Mrs Ericson over, Nils rejects the offer. Option **(c)**, then, is also incorrect.

Finally, we have **(d)**, which suggests that Nils spotted the woman whose home he is heading to. We know already that Nils is heading to Mrs Ericson's home. We know also that Mrs Ericson is the person driving the car that overtakes Nils and the farmer – 'Listen, if that ain't the old woman comin' now', the farmer says – and that Nils catches a glimpse of her driving 'bareheaded'. Option **(d)**, then, is the one that matches with the end of the passage, and is thus the correct answer.

Paper Eight: The Fisherman of Pass Christian

This extract is taken from a short story set in twentieth century Mississippi in the United States. Annette and Philip walk down to the pier that extends into the ocean.

1   The swift breezes on the beach at Pass Christian meet and conflict as though each strove for the mastery of the air. The land-breeze blows down through the pines, resinous, fragrant, cold, bringing breath-like memories of dim, dark woods shaded by myriad pine-needles. The breeze from the Gulf is warm and soft and languorous,
5   blowing up from the south with its suggestion of tropical warmth and passion. It is strong and masterful, and tossed Annette's hair and whipped her skirts about her in bold disregard for the proprieties.

Arm in arm with Philip, she was strolling slowly down the great pier which extends from the Mexican Gulf Hotel into the waters of the Sound. There was no moon to-
10   night, but the sky glittered and scintillated with myriad stars, brighter than you can ever see farther North, and the great waves that the Gulf breeze tossed up in restless profusion gleamed with the white fire of phosphorescent flame. The wet sands on the beach glowed white fire; the posts of the pier where the waves had leapt and left a laughing kiss, the sides of the little boats and fish-cars tugging at their ropes, alike
15   showed white and flaming, as though the sea and all it touched were afire.

Annette and Philip paused midway the pier to watch two fishermen casting their nets. With heads bared to the breeze, they stood in clear silhouette against the white background of sea.

"See how he uses his teeth," almost whispered Annette.

20 Drawing himself up to his full height, with one end of the huge seine between his teeth, and the cord in his left hand, the taller fisherman of the two paused a half instant, his right arm extended, grasping the folds of the net. There was a swishing rush through the air, and it settled with a sort of sob as it cut the waters and struck a million sparkles of fire from the waves. Then, with backs bending under the strain,
25 the two men swung on the cord, drawing in the net, laden with glittering restless fish, which were unceremoniously dumped on the boards to be put into the fish-car awaiting them.

Philip laughingly picked up a soft, gleaming jelly-fish, and threatened to put it on Annette's neck. She screamed, ran, slipped on the wet boards, and in another instant
30 would have fallen over into the water below. The tall fisherman caught her in his arms and set her on her feet.

"Mademoiselle must be very careful," he said in the softest and most correct French. "The tide is in and the water very rough. It would be very difficult to swim out there to-night."

35 Annette murmured confused thanks, which were supplemented by Philip's hearty tones. She was silent until they reached the pavilion at the end of the pier. The semi-darkness was unrelieved by lantern or light. The strong wind wafted the strains from a couple of mandolins, a guitar, and a tenor voice stationed in one corner to sundry engrossed couples in sundry other corners. Philip found an untenanted nook and they
40 ensconced themselves therein.

"Do you know there's something mysterious about that fisherman?" said Annette, during a lull in the wind.

"Because he did not let you go over?" inquired Philip.

"No; he spoke correctly, and with the accent that goes only with an excellent
45 education."

Philip shrugged his shoulders. "That's nothing remarkable. If you stay about Pass Christian for any length of time, you'll find more things than perfect French and courtly grace among fishermen to surprise you. These are a wonderful people who live across the Lake."

50 Annette was lolling in the hammock under the big catalpa-tree some days later, when the gate opened, and Natalie's big sun-bonnet appeared. Natalie herself was discovered blushing in its dainty depths. She was only a little Creole seaside girl, you must know, and very shy of the city demoiselles. Natalie's patois was quite as different from Annette's French as it was from the postmaster's English.

55   "Mees Annette," she began, peony-hued all over at her own boldness, "we will have one lil' hay-ride this night, and a fish-fry at the end. Will you come?"

Annette sprang to her feet in delight. "Will I come? Certainly. How delightful! You are so good to ask me. What shall—what time—" But Natalie's pink bonnet had fled precipitately down the shaded walk. Annette laughed joyously as Philip lounged down
60   the gallery.

"I frightened the child away," she told him.

An extract from Alice Dunbar Nelson's 'The fishermen of Pass Christian'

---

1. What time of the day is it at the start of this extract?

   a) Morning.
   b) Midday.
   c) Afternoon.
   d) Evening.

Answer: ___

2. What do we know about the weather conditions down on the pier?

   a) It is so hot as to make the sea seem like it is on fire.
   b) It is highly windy.
   c) It is raining lightly and there is a slight breeze.
   d) It is raining heavily and there is a slight breeze.

Answer: ___

3. 'The breeze from the Gulf is warm and soft and languorous, blowing up from the south with its suggestion of tropical warmth and passion.'

Which word is the proper noun in this sentence:

   a) Breeze.
   b) Gulf.
   c) South.
   d) Tropical.

Answer: ___

4. '[the breeze] whipped her skirts about her in bold disregard for the proprieties'

What does this mean?

    a) The breeze had no respect for Annette's property and clothes.
    b) The breeze had no respect for politeness in how it exposed Annette's body.
    c) The breeze had no respect for the fact it was making Annette cold.
    d) The breeze could be ignored if not for its impact on Annette's skirts.

Answer: ____

5. Which building does the great pier extend from?

    a) Pass Christian.
    b) The Mexican Gulf Hotel.
    c) The Sound Hotel.
    d) The Nook.

Answer: ____

6. 'scintillated with myriad stars'

What is another way of saying scintillated?

    a) Marvelled.
    b) Dizzied.
    c) Sparkled.
    d) Impressed.

Answer: ____

7. What would be another word for 'profusion' on line 12?

    a) Excitement.
    b) Profundity.
    c) Abundance.
    d) Energy.

Answer: ____

8. '[the waves] gleamed with the white fire of phosphorescent flame'

What does this suggest about the water?

a) That there was an oil slick on its surface that had caught fire.
b) There was a coral reef just below the surface that was glistening in the light.
c) The water was shining in such a way that it almost resembled white fire.
d) The water looked the exact opposite of a phosphorescent flame.

Answer: ___

9. 'The wet sands on the beach glowed white fire'

What technique is used in this phrase?

a) Litotes.
b) Personification.
c) Metaphor.
d) Simile.

Answer: ___

10. 'where the waves had leapt and left a laughing kiss'

This is an example of...

a) Personification.
b) Onomatopoeia.
c) Hyperbole.
d) Dehumanisation.

Answer: ___

11. Which word is the pronoun in the following sentence: 'With heads bared to the breeze, they stood in clear silhouette against the white background of sea.'

a) Heads.
b) Bared.
c) They.
d) Against.

Answer: ___

12. What is meant by 'silhouette'?

a) Outline.
b) Colour.
c) Sight.
d) Body.

Answer: ___

13. The writer describes the fish as 'restless'. What does this suggest about the fish?

a) They looked as though they were sleeping.
b) They appeared to be full of struggle and energy.
c) They seemed to be wrestling with each other.
d) They looked as though they were dead.

Answer: ___

14. 'unceremoniously dumped'

What does this say about the way the fishermen deposit the fish onto the pier?

a) They did so with solemn ritual.
b) They did so with tongue-in-cheek ritual.
c) They did so with the sadness of two men who had been dumped by their girlfriends.
d) They did so indelicately and without ritual.

Answer: ___

15. How are the fishermen planning to transport the fish they have caught away from the pier?

a) With the nets they used to catch them.
b) They are planning to release them back into the water.
c) With buckets.
d) With a fish-car.

Answer: ___

16. What type of word is 'gleaming' on line 28?

a) Adverb.
b) Pronoun.
c) Verb.
d) Adjective.

Answer: ___

17. What was Annette's reaction to Philip's attempt to place a jellyfish on her neck?

a) She whispered at Philip to stop.
b) She screamed and ran away.
c) She laughed and ran away.
d) She screamed and let him put the jellyfish on her.

Answer: ___

18. 'The tall fisherman caught her in his arms and set her on her feet'

How many adjectives can you count in the sentence above?

a) 1
b) 2
c) 3
d) 4

Answer: ___

19. If the fisherman had not caught Annette, where would she have fallen?

a) Into the water.
b) Into Philip's arms.
c) Into the second fisherman.
d) Onto the decking of the pier.

Answer: ___

20. What could Annette and Philip hear once they reached the pavilion?

a) Only the sound of mandolins.
b) Only the sound of others couples chatting.

c) Music and the sound of couples chatting.
d) Only the wind.

Answer: ___

21. Who else was in the 'nook' Annette and Philip entered at line 39?

a) Another couple engrossed in conversation.
b) A tenor singer.
c) A young girl called Natalie.
d) Nobody.

Answer: ___

22. Why does Annette find the fisherman who caught her mysterious?

a) Due to his unusually fast reactions.
b) Due to his educated accent and way of talking.
c) Due to his hypnotic fishing technique.
d) Due to the fact he is silent at all times.

Answer: ___

23. 'Philip shrugged his shoulders.'

What is the subject of the sentence?

a) Philip
b) Shrugged
c) His
d) Shoulders

Answer: ___

24. Why does Philip shrug his shoulders at Annette at line 46?

a) He also finds the fisherman mysterious – his shrug is one of confusion.
b) He finds the fisherman unexceptional – his shrug is one of casualness.
c) His shoulders are in pain and he is shrugging to let Annette know.
d) He is trying to warn Annette that they are not alone.

Answer: ___

25. What type of words are the following? 'almost' (line 19), 'slowly' (line 8), 'unceremoniously' (line 26), 'laughingly' (line 28), 'correctly' (line 44).

   a) Adverbs.
   b) Adjectives.
   c) Prepositions.
   d) Verbs.

Answer: ___

26. 'during a lull in the wind'

Which of the following words is closest in meaning to 'lull'?

   a) Escalation.
   b) Whistling.
   c) Pause.
   d) Gust.

Answer: ___

27. Where was Annette sitting when Natalie arrived?

   a) In a hammock.
   b) In a hollowed-out catalpa-tree.
   c) In medias res.
   d) In a nook.

Answer: ___

28. What type of words are the following? 'fragrant' (line 3), 'wet' (line 12), 'correct' (line 32), 'perfect' (line 47), 'dainty' (line 52).

   a) Verbs.
   b) Adverbs.
   c) Adjectives.
   d) Nouns.

Answer: ___

29. 'Natalie's patois was quite as different from Annette's French as it was from the postmaster's English.'

Which of the following words is closest in meaning to 'patois?

a) Accent.
b) Proficiency.
c) Dialect.
d) Vocabulary.

Answer: ___

30. Based on the passage, what is Natalie's main goal in paying Annette a visit?

a) To find out about the evening on the pier.
b) To invite Annette to a party.
c) To show Annette her new hat.
d) To deliver the post.

Answer: ___

31. What does the word 'peony-hued' suggest about Natalie in line 55?

a) It suggests she is blushing.
b) It suggests she looks like someone fond of ponies.
c) It suggests that she has gone very pale with shock.
d) It suggests she looks as pretty as a flower.

Answer: ___

32. 'Annette sprang to her feet in delight'

What is the object of this sentence?

a) Annette
b) Sprang
c) Feet
d) In

Answer: ___

33. Why does Natalie abruptly leave at the end of the extract?

a) She is rushing to invite others to the party.

b) She is startled by Annette's enthusiasm.

c) She is scared of the possibility of encountering Philip.

d) She is rushing to prepare food for the party.

Answer: ___

34. Which word does *not* describe Natalie?

a) Shy.

b) Jumpy.

c) Argumentative.

d) Intimidated.

Answer: ___

35. Which of these statements is true?

a) The tall fisherman speaks French.

b) Annette does not speak French.

c) Annette and Philip encounter three fisherman at the pier, all of whom speak French.

d) The tall fisherman speaks only in English.

Answer: ___

36. What tense is the opening paragraph written in?

a) Past tense.

b) Present tense.

c) Present tense then past tense.

d) Past tense then present tense.

Answer: ___

37. What tense are the final three paragraphs written in?

a) Past tense.

b) Present tense.

c) Present tense then past tense.

d) Past tense then present tense.

Answer: ___

38. Who is the narrator of this extract?

a) Annette.
b) Philip.
c) The fisherman.
d) None of the above.

Answer: ___

39. 'Annette laughed joyously as Philip lounged down the gallery'

Which word in this quote is a conjunction?

a) Laughed
b) As
c) Lounged
d) Down

Answer: ___

40. Which of these statements matches the end of the extract?

a) Natalie retracts her invitation to Annette.
b) Annette tells Philip about the invitation extended by Natalie.
c) Annette tells Philip that she frightened Natalie.
d) Annette invites Philip to the party.

Answer: ___

1. What time of the day is it at the start of this extract?

    a) Morning.
    b) Midday.
    c) Afternoon.
    d) Evening.

Answer: D

At lines 9-10 we learn that there 'was no moon to-night, but the sky glittered and scintillated with myriad stars'. Given that there are stars in the sky, we know that it is evening-time at the start of this extract, and so option (**d**) is correct.

2. What do we know about the weather conditions down on the pier?

    a) It is so hot as to make the sea seem like it is on fire.
    b) It is highly windy.
    c) It is raining lightly and there is a slight breeze.
    d) It is raining heavily and there is a slight breeze.

Answer: B

The correct answer here is (**b**): it is highly windy on the pier. In the very first sentence we are told of the 'swift breezes on the beach at Pass Christian' that 'meet and conflict as though each strove for the mastery of the air' – the word 'swift' implying that it is very breezy/windy, and the 'conflict' between the breezes implying a degree of intensity. We are also told the breeze from the Gulf 'is strong and masterful, and tossed Annette's hair and whipped her skirts', again suggesting intense breeze.

We know that both (**c**) and (**d**) are incorrect, as both claim that it is raining, yet there is no mention whatsoever of rain in this passage.

Although the sea *is* described as resembling fire in appearance as option (**a**) suggests, it is not a hot climate inducing this visual effect; it is the wind and the way it whips up the waves: 'the great waves that the Gulf breeze tossed up in restless profusion gleamed with the white fire of phosphorescent flame'. As a result, option (**a**) is incorrect.

3. 'The breeze from the Gulf is warm and soft and languorous, blowing up from the south with its suggestion of tropical warmth and passion.'

Which word is the proper noun in this sentence:

    a) Breeze.
    b) Gulf.
    c) South.
    d) Tropical.

Answer: B

Since (as I mentioned earlier earlier) a proper noun is a name given to a specific place, person or thing, we know the word 'Gulf' is the proper noun and (**b**) is the correct answer.

4. '[the breeze] whipped her skirts about her in bold disregard for the proprieties'

What does this mean?

    a) The breeze had no respect for Annette's property and clothes.

    b) **The breeze had no respect for politeness in how it exposed Annette's body.**

    c) **The breeze had no respect for the fact it was making Annette cold.**

    d) **The breeze could be ignored if not for its impact on Annette's skirts.**

Answer: B

The proprieties refer to the rules of politeness and manners observed by society and which are considered morally acceptable. This quote is personifying the wind and saying that, by whipping Annette's skirt up and exposing her private regions, it is breaking society's rules of politeness. Option (**b**), then, is the correct answer.

5. Which building does the great pier extend from?

    a) **Pass Christian.**
    b) **The Mexican Gulf Hotel.**
    c) **The Sound Hotel.**
    d) **The Nook.**

Answer: B

At lines 8-9, we are told that Annette and Philip stroll down 'the great pier which extends from the Mexican Gulf Hotel into the waters of the Sound'. The Mexican Gulf Hotel (option (**b**)), then, is the answer the examiner is looking for.

6. 'scintillated with myriad stars'

What is another way of saying scintillated?

    a) **Marvelled.**
    b) **Dizzied.**
    c) **Sparkled.**
    d) **Impressed.**

Answer: C

To scintillate is to flash or shimmer with light or to sparkle, so the correct answer here is **(c)**.

If you do not know the answer, it is always sensible to try and slot each of the choices into the sentence one by one to see which one seems to make the most sense, since this will allow you to make an educated guess. For instance, the phrase 'the sky glittered and marvelled with myriad stars' instantly does not feel right, so we can eliminate that and therefore better our odds of picking the right answer.

Moreover, if we take a moment to refer back to the extract and examine the context in greater detail – and not just depend on the small snippet that has been included in the question – we can see the writer also uses the word 'glittered' to describe the sky. If we did not know the meaning of the word 'scintillated', we might take a guess that it means something similar to 'glittered', and this again would point us towards **(c)**, 'sparkled'. This is not a fool proof tactic, but it is a method of making a more educated guess.

7. What would be another word for 'profusion' on line 12?

a) **Excitement.**
b) **Profundity.**
c) **Abundance.**
d) **Energy.**

Answer: C

If you have a profusion of something, it means you have a lot of it or an abundance, and so **(c)** is the correct answer.

As ever, it is sensible to look at the context in which the word appears – it's a good way to double check your answer, and essential if you do not know the meaning of the word.

8. '[the waves] gleamed with the white fire of phosphorescent flame'

What does this suggest about the water?

a) That there was an oil slick on its surface that had caught fire.

b) There was a coral reef just below the surface that was glistening in the light.

c) The water was shining in such a way that it almost resembled white fire.

d) The water looked the exact opposite of a phosphorescent flame.

Answer: C

The quote we are being asked about makes use of a metaphor: the water is being compared to fire, but without the use of 'like' or 'as'. The water is not *literally* on fire. Rather, the appearance of the water, and the way it gleams, is being described as resembling white fire – and so option **(c)** is the correct answer.

9. 'The wet sands on the beach glowed white fire'

What technique is used in this phrase?

a) Litotes.
b) Personification.
c) Metaphor.
d) Simile.

Answer: C

The sands on the beach are not *literally* on fire; rather, they are being compared to 'white fire'. Yet, crucially, the comparison is implicit – that is, the author does not make use of either 'like' or 'as'. As such, we know this is a metaphor as opposed to a simile, and thus **(c)** is correct.

Of the other options above, the word 'litotes' is not one we have come across before. It refers to the use of deliberate understatement. For example, if wanted to express the fact you liked something, and you said 'hey, that's not too bad at all', this would be an instance of litotes. However, since it is not being employed here, **(a)** is also incorrect.

· · ·

10. 'where the waves had leapt and left a laughing kiss'

This is an example of...

　　a) **Personification.**
　　b) **Onomatopoeia.**
　　c) **Hyperbole.**
　　d) **Dehumanisation.**

Answer: A

Given that the waves here are described as though they are alive and delivering 'a laughing kiss', and this is an instance of personification, we know option **(a)** is the correct answer.

We have covered onomatopoeia a number of times and can see that it is not present in this quote (thereby eliminating **(b)**).

Hyperbole means something very similar to exaggeration; so if the writer had written that 'the waves had leapt higher than the gods themselves could have tossed them', this would have been an example of hyperbole. However, since there is no such hyperbole present here, **(c)** is also incorrect.

Dehumanisation is when a human being is described in a way that seems to take away their humanity. For example, if I described someone as a dog, I would be dehumanising them. In some respects, it might be considered the complete opposite of personification; and seeing as it is definitely not present in the above quote, **(d)** is also incorrect.

11. Which word is the pronoun in the following sentence: 'With heads bared to the breeze, they stood in clear silhouette against the white background of sea.'

　　a) **Heads**
　　b) **Bared**
　　c) **They**
　　d) **Against**

Answer: C

As mentioned earlier, a pronoun is a word that substitutes in for proper noun(s) in certain contexts, and examples include 'he', 'she', 'they', 'him', 'she', 'them', and so on. Option **(c)**, then, is the correct answer here, since 'they' is substituting in for 'Philip and Annette'.

12. What is meant by 'silhouette'?

    a) Outline.
    b) Colour.
    c) Sight.
    d) Body.

Answer: A

Someone's silhouette is the outline you can see of them when there is not quite enough light to see them clearly, so **(a)** is the correct answer.

13. The writer describes the fish as 'restless'. What does this suggest about the fish?

    a) They looked as though they were sleeping.
    b) They appeared to be full of struggle and energy.
    c) They seemed to be wrestling with each other.
    d) They looked as though they were dead.

Answer: B

To be restless is to be full of energy, or to be engaged in constant activity. Of the options above, **(b)** best captures what this word says about the fish – namely, that they appeared to be full of struggle and energy.

Option **(c)** is trying to exploit the fact that restless sounds a bit like wrestle to try and confuse us. However, the two words are different and do not mean the same thing, so **(c)** is not correct.

14. 'unceremoniously dumped'

What does this say about the way the fishermen deposit the fish onto the pier?

    a) **They did so with solemn ritual.**
    b) **They did so with tongue-in-cheek ritual.**
    c) **They did so with the sadness of two men who had been dumped by their girlfriends.**
    d) **They did so indelicately and without ritual.**

Answer: D

To do something unceremoniously means to do it without ritual or ceremony; in other words, in a kind of casual, fairly uncaring way. Moreover, if you dump something, it suggests you are putting it down or depositing it without much care or delicacy. The definition of phrase tallies with option **(d)** – the correct answer.

15. How are the fishermen planning to transport the fish they have caught away from the pier?

    a) **With the nets they used to catch them.**
    b) **They are planning to release them back into the water.**
    c) **With buckets.**
    d) **With a fish-car.**

Answer: D

At lines 26-27 we are told that the fish are 'unceremoniously dumped on the boards to be put into the fish-car awaiting them'. Since the 'fish-car' is awaiting them, it is logical to infer that this is the mode of transport the fishermen are planning to use to transport the fish, so **(d)** is correct.

16. What type of word is 'gleaming' on line 28?

    a) **Adverb.**
    b) **Pronoun.**
    c) **Verb.**

d) Adjective.

Answer: D

At line 28 we are told that 'Philip laughingly picked up a soft, gleaming jelly-fish'. The word 'gleaming', then, is being used to describe a noun ('jelly-fish'), and is thus an adjective. As such, option (**d**) is correct.

17. What was Annette's reaction to Philip's attempt to place a jellyfish on her neck?

    a) She whispered at Philip to stop.
    b) She screamed and ran away.
    c) She laughed and ran away.
    d) She screamed and let him put the jellyfish on her.

Answer: B

At line 27 we learn that, after Philip threatens to put the jellyfish on Annette, she 'screamed, ran, slipped on the wet boards'. None of the options above mention the fact she slipped. However, option (**b**) does correctly note that she screamed and ran away, and it is therefore the best answer available to us.

18. 'The tall fisherman caught her in his arms and set her on her feet'

How many adjectives can you count in the sentence above?

    a) 1
    b) 2
    c) 3
    d) 4

Answer: A

There is in fact just one adjective in this sentence: 'tall'. As such, **(a)** is the correct answer.

19. If the fisherman had not caught Annette, where would she have fallen?

    a) **Into the water.**
    b) **Into Philip's arms.**
    c) **Into the second fisherman.**
    d) **Onto the decking of the pier.**

Answer: A

At lines 27-28 we learn that, if it had not been for the fisherman, 'in another instant [Annette] would have fallen over into the water below'. Option **(a)**, then, is the correct answer.

20. What could Annette and Philip hear once they reached the pavilion?

    a) **Only the sound of mandolins.**
    b) **Only the sound of others couples chatting.**
    c) **Music and the sound of couples chatting.**
    d) **Only the wind.**

Answer: C

Let's take a look at lines 37 to 39, which is when Annette and Philip reach the pavilion: 'The strong wind wafted the strains from a couple of mandolins, a guitar, and a tenor voice stationed in one corner to sundry engrossed couples in sundry other corners'.

We can see that they hear not only mandolins – a type of instrument – but also a 'guitar' and a singer ('tenor voice'), as well as the sound of 'engrossed couples' talking. Accordingly, option **(c)** is correct.

21. Who else was in the 'nook' Annette and Philip entered at line 39?

a) **Another couple engrossed in conversation.**
b) **A tenor singer.**
c) **A young girl called Natalie.**
d) **Nobody**.

Answer: D

At lines 39-40 we are told 'Philip found an untenanted nook and they ensconced themselves therein'. If something is untenanted, it means it is uninhabited, and thus this quote indicates that option (**d**) – which suggests nobody was in the nook – is correct.

The other couples in conversation and the tenor singer can both be heard prior to Annette and Philip entering the nook, but they are not in fact in the nook, and thus (**a**) and (**b**) are both incorrect. Moreover, Natalie does not appear on that evening at all; she appears a number of days later near the end of the extract, and this therefore invalidates option (**c**).

22. Why does Annette find the fisherman who caught her mysterious?

a) **Due to his unusually fast reactions.**
b) **Due to his educated accent and way of talking.**
c) **Due to his hypnotic fishing technique.**
d) **Due to the fact he is silent at all times.**

Answer: B

At lines 44-45, Annette tells Philip why she finds the fisherman mysterious: 'He spoke correctly, and with the accent that goes only with an excellent education'. In short, it was the fisherman's manner of talking, which seemed to connote an 'excellent education', that Annette found mysterious; ergo: option (**b**) is the correct answer.

23. 'Philip shrugged his shoulders.'

What is the subject of the sentence?

a) **Philip**

b) Shrugged
c) His
d) Shoulders

Answer: A

The subject of a sentence, we know, is the person or thing that is doing or being. Philip is the one shrugging his shoulders, hence Philip (option **(a)**) is the subject of the sentence.

24. Why does Philip shrug his shoulders at Annette at line 46?

    a) He also finds the fisherman mysterious – his shrug is one of confusion.
    b) He finds the fisherman unexceptional – his shrug is one of casualness.
    c) His shoulders are in pain and he is shrugging to let Annette know.
    d) He is trying to warn Annette that they are not alone.

Answer: B

Immediately after Annette explains why she finds the fisherman mysterious, Philip shrugs and says 'that's nothing remarkable', before explaining that in this area there are 'more things than perfect French and courtly grace among fishermen' that ought to surprise anyone. His tone, then, is nonchalant (casual), and he is shrugging because he finds the fisherman's manner of speaking unexceptional. In light of all this, we can plainly see that **(b)** is the correct answer.

25. What type of words are the following? 'almost' (line 19), 'slowly' (line 8), 'unceremoniously' (line 26), 'laughingly' (line 28), 'correctly' (line 44).

    a) Adverbs.
    b) Adjectives.
    c) Prepositions.

d) Verbs.

Answer: A

These words are all adverbs, since, if you go and look at each of them in context, you can see that each and every one is used to describe a verbs. Option (**a**), then, is the correct answer.

26. 'during a lull in the wind'

Which of the following words is closest in meaning to 'lull'?

a) **Escalation.**
b) **Whistling.**
c) **Pause.**
d) **Gust.**

Answer: C

A lull is a temporary pause or cessation in something. The author, here, is saying that there was a momentary pause in the wind. As such, option (**c**) is correct.

27. Where was Annette sitting when Natalie arrived?

a) **In a hammock.**
b) **In a hollowed-out catalpa-tree.**
c) **In medias res.**
d) **In a nook.**

Answer: A

At line 50 we learn that Annette was 'lolling in the hammock' when 'Natalie's big sun-bonnet appeared'. To loll means to sit or lie somewhere (not to be confused with the slang phrase "lol"), and thus we are being told that Annette was resting in the hammock when Natalie arrives. Option (**a**), then, is correct.

. . .

28. What type of words are the following? 'fragrant' (line 3), 'wet' (line 12), 'correct' (line 32), 'perfect' (line 47), 'dainty' (line 52).

   a) Verbs.
   b) Adverbs.
   c) Adjectives.
   d) Nouns.

Answer: C

All of these words are used to describe nouns, and, as such, are adjectives (option **(c)**).

29. 'Natalie's patois was quite as different from Annette's French as it was from the postmaster's English.'

Which of the following words is closest in meaning to 'patois?

   a) Accent.
   b) Proficiency.
   c) Dialect.
   d) Vocabulary.

Answer: C

The word 'patois' refers to a kind of regional dialect – and usually it refers to a dialect used by a group of people who are not especially powerful in the society within which they exist. Indeed, it refers to something more extensive than just a different accent; it refers to a unique way of speaking that is peculiar to a particular region or group of people. As such, option **(c)** is correct.

30. Based on the passage, what is Natalie's main goal in paying Annette a visit?

   a) To find out about the evening on the pier.
   b) To invite Annette to a party.

c) To show Annette her new hat.
d) To deliver the post.

Answer: B

Natalie only speaks once in this passage – at lines 55 to 56 – and the answer to this question resides in this one instance of dialogue: "'Mees Annette," she began, peony-hued all over at her own boldness, "we will have one lil' hay-ride this night, and a fish-fry at the end. Will you come?'"

It appears that Natalie is informing Annette that there will be a 'hay-ride' and a 'fish-fry' – leisure activities and food – that evening, and is asking whether Annette would like to come. Insofar as a party might be described as a leisurely social gathering, it would appear that **(b)** is correct: Natalie's main goal in paying Annette a visit is to invite her to a party.

31. What does the word 'peony-hued' suggest about Natalie in line 55?

    a) It suggests she is blushing.
    b) It suggests she looks like someone fond of ponies.
    c) It suggests that she has gone very pale with shock.
    d) It suggests she looks as pretty as a flower.

Answer: A

A peony is a pink flower, whereas to the word 'hue' means something like colour; so, in short, we are being told that she has gone pink; and from this, we can infer that Natalie is blushing, and that **(a)** is correct.

However, if we hadn't known that peonies were pink, we could have still eliminated options and placed ourselves in a better position to guess. We are told that the shy Natalie, after addressing Annette, became 'peony-hued all over at her own boldness'. Options **(b)** and **(d)**, which seem to be unrelated to how Natalie's boldness might impact on her appearance, can quickly be eliminated.

It's true that, if one did not know that peony-hued implied she had gone pink/was blushing, one might think she may have gone pale with shock **(c)**. Nevertheless, by narrowing down our choices, we give ourselves a better chance of guessing!

· · ·

32. 'Annette sprang to her feet in delight'

What is the object of this sentence?

a) **Annette**
b) **Sprang**
c) **Feet**
d) **In**

Answer: C

The object of the sentence is the person or thing on the receiving end of the verb. Annette's feet are on the receiving end of the verb ('sprang'), and thus **(c)** is correct – 'feet' is the object of the sentence.

33. Why does Natalie abruptly leave at the end of the extract?

a) **She is rushing to invite others to the party.**
b) **She is startled by Annette's enthusiasm.**
c) **She is scared of the possibility of encountering Philip.**
d) **She is rushing to prepare food for the party.**

Answer: B

Let's take a look at the section of the extract that deals with Natalie's abrupt departure:

'Annette sprang to her feet in delight. "Will I come? Certainly. How delightful! You are so good to ask me. What shall—what time—" But Natalie's pink bonnet had fled precipitately down the shaded walk.'

We are not told explicitly in this quoted section what causes Natalie to depart. However, given the order of events – Annette springs to her feet (the word 'sprang' implying high energy) and issues an impassionedly enthusiastic response (as signified by the exclamation marks and the dashes); then, immediately after, Natalie flees – one can infer that it was Annette's explosive enthusiasm that scared Natalie off. This tallies closely with option (**b**).

A further clue that (**b**) is the option the examiner is seeking is the fact that it also matches Annette's own assessment of what induced Natalie to flee: 'I frightened the child away'.

34. Which word does *not* describe Natalie?

a) Shy.
b) Jumpy.
c) Argumentative.
d) Intimidated.

Answer: C

As indicated earlier, our best bet with this particular style of question is the process of elimination.

We know Natalie is shy, because we are told at line 53 that she is 'very shy of the city demoiselles', so we can eliminate (**a**).

To be jumpy is to be easily startled. When Annette responds to Natalie's invitation with enthusiasm, Natalie runs away in a state of startlement: 'But Natalie's pink bonnet had fled precipitately down the shaded walk'. As a result, we could definitely characterise Natalie as jumpy, so (**b**) is incorrect.

To be argumentative is to be prone to picking fights and arguing with others. Natalie, however, does not argue with anyone in this extract. On the contrary: at the first sign of heightened emotions, she runs away. So it would seem (**c**) does not apply to Natalie, and is thus likely our correct answer.

Finally, we have option (**d**), intimidated; and, sure enough, Natalie does very much seem to be intimated by Annette – so much so that she runs away when Annette excitedly responds to Natalie's invitation. This confirms that (**c**) is the correct answer.

35. Which of these statements is true?

a) The tall fisherman speaks French.
b) Annette does not speak French.

c) Annette and Philip encounter three fisherman at the pier, all of whom speak French.

d) The tall fisherman speaks only in English.

Answer: A

At line 32, just after the taller fisherman catches Annette, we have the following text: '"Mademoiselle must be very careful," he said in the softest and most correct French.'

Although we, as readers, are given the English translation of what the fisherman said, it is made very clear that he had spoken these words in 'the softest and most correct French'. Accordingly, option **(a)** must be the correct answer: the tall fisherman does indeed speak French.

36. What tense is the opening paragraph written in?

a) **Past tense.**
b) **Present tense.**
c) **Present tense then past tense.**
d) **Past tense then present tense.**

Answer: C

This is one of the trickiest questions in this entire guide.

Every sentence in the opening paragraph aside from the final one is in fact written in the present tense. Let's look at the second sentence, for example, which starts with 'the land-breeze blows down through the pines'. Now, the verb 'blows' here is clearly placing us in the present tense – if it had been written in the past tense, the author would have used 'blew' instead. To illustrate further, let's look at the start of the third sentence: 'The breeze from the Gulf is warm and soft and languorous'. If the author had used the word 'was' instead of 'is', we would have been in the past tense; but she has instead used the word 'is', which places us in the present tense.

However, whereas most of the opening paragraph is written in the present tense, the final sentence differs: 'It is strong and masterful, and tossed Annette's hair and whipped her skirts about her in bold disregard for the proprieties'.

The very start of the sentence appears to still be written in the present tense: we are told the breeze 'is strong and masterful' – again, the word 'is' has been used instead of 'was'. Yet we are then told that it 'tossed Annette's hair and whipped her skirts', and 'tossed' and 'whipped' both imply past tense (the author would have had to use 'tosses' and 'whips' to maintain the present tense).

So, to conclude, the first paragraph starts in the present tense, and ends in the past tense, and, consequently, **(c)** is correct.

37. What tense are the final three paragraphs written in?

  a) **Past tense.**
  b) **Present tense.**
  c) **Present tense then past tense.**
  d) **Past tense then present tense.**

Answer: A

After the opening paragraph, the author remains in the past tense throughout the rest of the extract – including in the final three paragraphs – and thus **(a)** is correct.

I would definitely recommend that, when presented with a question of this kind, you ought to go the extra mile of quickly re-reading the 'mini-passage' referenced in the question – if only to ensure that there are no nuances that you did not notice the first time round!

38. Who is the narrator of this extract?

  a) **Annette.**
  b) **Philip.**
  c) **The fisherman.**
  d) **None of the above.**

Answer: D

The correct answer is **(d)**, since the extract is written in the third person, and not by any one character.

. . .

39. 'Annette laughed joyously as Philip lounged down the gallery'

Which word in this quote is a conjunction?

   a) **Laughed**
   b) **As**
   c) **Lounged**
   d) **Down**

Answer: B

You may recall from earlier in this guide that a conjunction is a word that is used to connect words, phrases, clauses or sentences, and that examples include 'but', 'and', 'because', 'so', 'whether' and 'yet'.

When we use 'as' to communicate two events unfolding at the same time, it functions as a conjunction, and thus **(b)** is the correct answer here.

40. Which of these statements matches the end of the extract?

   a) **Natalie retracts her invitation to Annette.**
   b) **Annette tells Philip about the invitation extended by Natalie.**
   c) **Annette tells Philip that she frightened Natalie.**
   d) **Annette invites Philip to the party.**

Answer: C

At the very end of the extract, Annette tells Philip that she had frightened Natalie off: '"I frightened the child away," she told him.' Accordingly, **(c)** is the correct answer.